Nothing's for Nothing

Transformation Through Trauma

Rebekah Demirel

ROSE HIP PRESS

Nothing's for Nothing
Transformation Through Trauma

PUBLISHED BY

ROSE HIP
PRESS

Seattle, Washington
www.rosehippress.com

COVER & INTERIOR DESIGN

Bob Lanphear
www.LanphearDesign.com

Library of Congress Cataloging-in-Publication Data
Demirel, Rebekah
Nothing's for nothing/Rebekah Demirel.

ISBN: 978-0-9970368-5-5

For my mother Mary

When I find myself in times of trouble,
mother Mary comes to me...

A Note from Rose Hip Press

Rose Hip Press is delighted and proud to introduce Rebekah Demirel's remarkable memoir, *Nothing's for Nothing*. As Gabor Maté observes in this book's Foreword, tragedy and pain may be inevitable, but healing is not. Which is why we need stories like Rebekah's: searing, yet hopeful, unflinching in describing painful realities, but equally honest about the love to be found in even the most fractured families. A noted trauma specialist and acupuncturist, Rebekah is also a wonderful writer with a gift for delineating the fine borders between ordinary pain and poetic insight.

Like the rose hip—a wild medicinal plant—Rebekah's stories are a healing resource accessible to anyone willing to approach their own lives with her brave compassion and curiosity. Readers will find their own most difficult experiences reflected in these stories, but it is Rebekah Demirel's unforgettable voice—intimate, funny, sad, full of wonder—which conveys such a feeling of what it's like to heal, to become more whole.

Contents

Acknowledgments

I wrote most of this memoir over a year's time, then took another year deciding to edit and publish it. Certainly, without the encouragement and support of some key people, I think it'd still be locked up in my brain and heart.

With this book, and like many things I've done in life, I can honestly say that what I lack in polish and skill, I will always do my best to balance with enthusiasm. I am blessed to be surrounded by people who see this and love me for who I am, warts and all.

Many people have been with me on this project from the beginning, before I even knew it would be a book. One of my most faithful readers has been Carol Poole, who ever since reading my first article in *Crosscut* about my teen years on the streets, has offered kind words of encouragement for me to write more, inspiring me with her own memoir, *Grits, Green Beans and the Holy Ghost*, which my husband read to me as a bedtime story each night, often moving us both to tears. Thank you Carol, for how your heart goes into everything you say and do. And thank you for the honor of making this the second memoir to be published by Rose Hip Press.

Sincere thanks to the talented, kind-hearted, skillful and patient designer, Bob Lanphear, who not only created a beautiful cover and compelling layout for the book, but who constantly surprised me with how he so personally and respectfully cared about helping me, this babe-in-the-woods writer, feel good about the whole process. Thank you, Bob! You are a rare and wonderful person.

For everyone who read parts of this manuscript in its raw form, including many friends, family and people I've never met who wrote me with comments of appreciation, I thank you. I even discovered that the stories from my blog, where this book began, were read in sixteen different countries over the first year of my writing it, which touched and surprised me! I am so truly grateful for you all taking the time to read and reflect on things I've written. Special thanks to Rex Hohlebein, Rev. Rick Reynolds and Gina Salá for their endorsements and kind support.

To Gabor Maté, my friend and colleague, whose gentle validation of what was difficult for me to speak about, helped plant the early seeds of what I'd eventually write. Thank you for your very generous words of praise written in the foreword for this book, which I will try to accept with grace and without self-deprecation. It was you who said to me, "Your blog is eighty thousand words? That's a book!" So much of how I've grown as a person has been inspired by your lifelong commitment to truth and healing and I am grateful to know you and to call you friend.

I am grateful to all of my friends and family, many of whom I've mentioned in the stories, some of whom are not living on this earth any more. I thank you all for the lessons you continue to teach me. Without you, there would be no book.

Finally, to my husband Sinan, who not only stands by me through all of my rants, raves, and moments of unreasonable expectations and disappointments, but who has listened to countless iterations of my stories, with a kind, yet critical ear. As the editor of this book, your smart heart and keen eye have combed through each word so that I could say all I held inside in the most authentic way. I know you do all these things because you love me and I am grateful beyond what I can ever express.

To everyone: Thank you for believing that I have something to say. May we all learn to live in peace together.

Foreword

Not for nothing did my friend and colleague Rebekah Demirel write *Nothing's for Nothing*. The project began as a series of blogs in which Rebekah chronicled the *feel* of her life, feelings that came up for her day to day and the memories attached to those feelings.

The memories were laid down long ago, during a childhood troubled by a hostile divorce between a vindictive father and a mother marginalized and eventually forced into absence, a childhood also characterized by poverty, abuse, the ghost-like haunting of a jailed brother who eventually dies a stranger. Addiction, dysfunction, depression, self-loathing, and dysfunctional relationship inevitably followed.

Not inevitable but self-wrought was the healing that came in the wake of all these miseries, healing that Rebekah courageously and doggedly pursued, worked at and achieved for herself and which she shares now so gracefully and skillfully with her clients and students, as I have personally witnessed.

In the story fragments she records in this book Rebekah evokes the memories of past miseries and struggles, but always as a way of stepping into the present with power and humor. "Though most things are not messy anymore for me," she writes, "I still don't mind the messy parts in my life – a bit of chaos, a touch of something unexpected, an experience that may even seem like a mistake... God bless this mess."

As that vignette shows, Rebekah's greatest gift in this charming volume is resilience. She truly is one of the most resilient people I know, and her writing conveys that effortlessly. The book is a collection of brief recollections and cogent, succinct thoughts regarding the lessons derived from those memories. The resilience resides in those lessons, but even more in the very lightness with which Rebekah touches upon her own—and the reader's—pain. Under her deft touch (and it truly is an expert touch, that of an adept practitioner of Chinese medicine and acupuncture), pain becomes not a source of defeat but of liberation.

Far from all the memories are those of trauma—nothing traumatic, for example, about pizza on Hornby Island! So this book is about a life, a life if not always lived consciously, then remembered consciously in a way that makes the reader more alive and aware. The child evoked in its pages may not have known it, but every experience she endured or enjoyed had a purpose, as all our lives do once we commit to learning and growth. Truly not for nothing.

Gabor Maté M.D.
Author, *In The Realm of Hungry Ghosts: Close Encounters With Addiction*

Preface

About a year ago, I began to chronicle my childhood stories in a blog called Integratefull. Recollecting them in no particular order, I made myself sit down every day and let my hands start moving on the keyboard.

The memories were not always pleasant or happy, and I found that through writing and allowing things to arise, I was processing trauma. Some long-held beliefs started to change, and without setting out to do so, I was integrating the experiences and making peace with my past.

Often, when I dredged up what had lain dormant in my psyche, I became nauseated and dizzy. I'd have to get up, breathe, and remind myself that I was safe, right in that moment, and then the feelings would pass. My body was reliving things I'd stowed away for decades, which was cathartic – though at the same time, I had to be sensitive and pace myself.

When moments of doubt, fear and sorrow emerged, I remembered a quote from Jesus in the Gospel of Thomas. He said: "If you bring forth what is within you, what you bring forth will save you. If you do not bring forth what is within you, what you do not bring forth will destroy you."

I figured that "bringing it forth" was one of the most useful things I could do with what I'd experienced in my life, so this book is about precisely that: letting it out, letting it go, and noticing what insight is left when the dust settles.

Something else I've learned from this journey of self-discovery is that what happened and what I do with it are connected but different. Our experiences are at the root of our thoughts and actions, they inform our choices, but they don't have to determine how we respond to life.

Here's an example: If I experienced loss, like my mother leaving our home when I was three, an idea might have formed, even way back then. The idea might be something like: "If I love someone, they will leave me." After all, I have the evidence for this idea, because Mom did leave, so I feel justified in having this belief.

I can also start to tell myself, "It is not safe to love anyone, because they will leave and I will be hurt." Now lots of other ideas and beliefs can form: "There is something wrong, flawed, lacking in me, which is why no one will love me. There is no use even trying to love and be loved. It doesn't work and it never will. I am unlovable…"

Trust me; these are some of the tricks my mind played on me. I lived for decades believing my stressful thoughts, until I began to see that none of those beliefs were ever true in the first place.

It's sobering, but also liberating, to know we have choices about our thoughts and beliefs, while other things in life may be much harder to change.

My dad, for all his faults, taught me an important lesson when I was bullied at school for being poor, smelly and shoddily dressed. He'd tell me to ignore the bullies and be kindest to the other kids who were bullied or ignored. I did that as much from wanting friendship as sharing the solidarity of exclusion with them.

I also realize that even with the hardships in my life, I've had many built-in advantages like being white, considered pretty by conventional societal standards, and, unlike my brother, I was not the one being sexually abused at home by our father. I was the one witnessing his abuse, so a sense of survivor guilt has been part of my collateral damage.

What I do know is there were, and still are, multiple factors that enable me to move through society's obstacles more easily than many other people. For me this knowledge comes with a responsibility to be generous with my time, stand against discrimination and inequality, and for inclusion, opportunity and community for everyone.

And even when it's really hard to be kind, like when others aren't, I may not always succeed, but I still try my best to take the high road and be kind anyhow, because that's when kindness is needed most.

I offer my stories and insights, sharing here some of the messy, often foolish, ways I've found grace in the most unlikely places. And though I started the blog as a sort of journal, with no real order to the stories, I've arranged them here roughly chronologically so that it's easier to follow.

Some of the memories I touch on are indelible and still fresh, like they happened yesterday, and for these stories the images are clear and easy to recall. Other times, it's been more difficult to bring forth some of the more painful recollections, knowing I've psychically put them aside, but even so, I've tried to keep opening.

I've changed some people's names, to protect their privacy, but all of the stories are true, as true as I can remember them. And without intending to do so, I notice that I have written many of the childhood stories in a childlike way, speaking in the voice of a child in some parts. I guess this must have been necessary for me to access the memories and express them as authentically as I could.

My sister Nora and I had the same parents and much of the same types of childhood trauma, even though we were born almost twenty years apart. We share the pain, as well as some of the good things we have both inherited.

Other family members, like my dad, mom and brother David, are gone now and I haven't spoken to my brother Michael in years, though I hope that we will be able to talk again one day and start to heal some of the trauma we experienced together as children.

I have tried to be very respectful of Michael in particular, not using his real name or describing him in detail. Though he may never read this book, I hope that if he does, it could help him to know I think of him, that I acknowledge his suffering and mostly, that I wish him well.

Sprinkled throughout this book, you'll find italicized passages where I delve into some of my personal insights gained through deep psychological and spiritual work. And since I am an acupuncturist and East Asian medicine practitioner, there are also a few musings from my personal familiarity with being both a patient and provider of acupuncture, qi gong and herbal medicine, for which I will be forever grateful.

There are certain key experiences that I relive more than once in the text, seeking to understand how I have been affected, and thus how I've lived. One such key experience is when my mother left, then came back to take her children with her, only for us to be later taken back by my father.

Much of my angst has come down to a moment in time, where I have traced a lot of my struggle with decision-making, guilt and shame. Seeing where the struggle started, I choose to keep working to untangle all the knots and let the light in.

While reading this book, start from the beginning, or jump in at any point, but whichever you choose, may you enjoy the ride – laugh, cry, and have your own moments of realization along the way.

And since our addictions, compulsions and tightly held ways of living all started somewhere, I hope you find, like I did, that being curious and continuing to uncover ourselves helps to squeeze the richness from life.

My dearest wish is that what I have written might inspire you to dig deep, to express and bring forth what is in you.

Like my mom used to say, "Nothing's for Nothing," which I think means everything has a purpose, though there also seems to be a Zen koan-like riddle hidden in "Nothing's for Nothing" that could beg the question ... so what is nothing for?

PART I

IT WAS A MESS
AND SO WERE WE

You...

Early memories of you gather in my mind and heart. How did I get to love you, resent you, and long for you for so many years? ... Just a few precious flickers before you left when I was three.

Loud voices wake me, you and my dad are yelling at each other and then I am crying, wandering to the kitchen. My dad tells me it's okay, as he sits me on the high pink stool and makes me raisin toast. You come into the room then you leave quickly. No kiss for me to dry my tears.

Another time, we sit together on the porch, on a sultry summer day. You, with one leg stretched out in the sun's warmth. I am lolling in your lap, smelling the cotton freshness of your dress. All is well. All is perfect. Your fingers are entwined in my curls, laid against my skull. There is nowhere better than this.

I have no idea what you are thinking just then, as you touch my dewy skin, feeling the weight of me on your thighs. You are grieving already, wondering if you will leave, wondering how you can take me with you, or how you could leave me here.

There are some things you can never forget and even this tender moment is stained by what you would rather not remember...You are eight months pregnant with me, he is angry, yelling. He holds a butcher knife to your belly, to me, to us and threatens: "I could cut you right now and get that thing out of you."

After that, it was impossible for you to stay because you could never feel safe again. You weaned me and left. We will both carry the scar for years to come.

But here, in this serene moment, my face is tipped upward. A deep humming purrs in my chest, or is that your heartbeat? I stare at the brightness, your face, the sun, your face, the sun ... It calls me. You call me. Impossibly, I hear the sun buzzing, too loud. My head throbs like it will burst.

"Stop looking at it," you say. "You will burn your eyes. Close your eyes Sweetie!"

I'm torn from it by you, scooped up and put to bed, bathed with a cold cloth, like I am ill with a fever, but I only want to go back to that moment with you, that perfect moment of utter envelopment.

Then you are gone and I am left there, not knowing where you are. An eternity goes by without you. Once or twice more you come to see your children, but you are turned away. I am later chastised by daddy for singing to you. I sang "Robin in the Rain," like you'd taught me. I wanted to see you smile.

Once you did manage to take us with you, but that only lasts a very short while before he comes to get us and then you are gone again.

Years and years pass and life somehow goes on without you until ...

I am twelve and I decide it's time to see you. Aunt Hazel knows where you are, gives me your number to call.

"Mom?"

"Where are you?"

"At home."

"Can I see you?"

"Meet me at the ballpark by our house tomorrow after school," I say, and then hang up, my heart pounding. I don't dare breathe a word of our secret meeting to anyone. I am as excited as I am anxious.

I would have known you from ten miles away. Your hair is a big fuzzy ball of blonde, those lips – hot pink, pink nails, too, and a leopard-print coat. Perfumed from head to toe. Not like the church ladies. Not like my aunties or Grandma. Not like any of my friends' moms.

You are more like a movie star, the kind my dad always sneers at on TV, one of those wicked women men always want. Ginger from *Gilligan's Island*.

You are exactly how I imagined you all these years.

I want to loll in your lap again, sitting here on the baseball bleachers in the sun. I want to put my head against your chest, hear your heartbeat, dig my fingers into your clouds of hair …

Instead I kick the dirt, feeling scruffy and unworthy of your magnificence.

I want to ask, "Where were you? Why didn't you come back again? Why didn't you try harder to take me with you? Where were you?"

Instead I am sullen, withdrawn and silent.

After a while you get up to leave. "I can come again and we can go bowling or something."

"Yeah, okay," I mumble.

"Can you come give your mother a kiss?"

My arms and legs move all at once, and I am swallowed in a honeysuckle embrace. Pink lipstick smears my cheeks and I am giddy, spinning, sunlight laughing, all in an instant of having you again. I will myself to let go of you, to compose myself.

"See you again soon, then?" you ask.

"Yeah. Okay," I say. "Bye."

Walking away, I look back over my shoulder a couple of times, before you disappear over the hill. Each time I look back, you are looking back, too.

Sunshine hums in my ears. My chest feels like flying.

Messy

So much in my life has been messy, tripping along through bad choices leading to disastrous and dangerous situations and just making, well, a mess of things. I didn't know what else to do.

The house I grew up in was not only messy, but it was also filthy, a background to the unsanitary chaos of my childhood. After Mom left, my dad was angry and depressed, my six-year-old brother was devastated, and I was three years old, stunned and bereft. So any efforts by us to keep the house clean all went out the door when Mom did. It was a mess and so were we.

The divorce was messy, too. In court, my dad called Mom "unfit" to be our mother (she would tell me years later). He got relatives and people from the church to testify that she was "irresponsible and immoral," so he won sole custody of us. Then, to add injury to insult, there was a restraining order that kept her from her children; that part was the meanest, the most devastating.

In desperation, Mom later "kidnapped" (the word my dad used) us to live with her, but that plan was soon foiled when we were found and taken back to live with our father. It was nine more years till I saw her again, and my brother, Michael, took some more time, eventually reuniting with Mom, though there was a lot that was broken between them that might never heal.

Two sad, stressed kids, shortly before Mom left. Dad and Aunt Hazel, Mom holding me

My dad marshalling so much support for his case to keep a mother from her children seems particularly cruel, and the shame and powerlessness projected on Mom by the court proceedings was certainly his intention. What my dad didn't realize was how much the messy divorce and custody battle would hurt his children even more.

I have some clear memories of how things deteriorated and got much messier once Mom was gone. Paint peeled; black, moldering slime grew on windowsills; slugs appeared around the toilet and tub, thinking that so warm and fecund a place must be home. Newspapers piled up on my old high chair in the bathroom, now repurposed as "the reading room," as my dad called it, since it was where he'd sit and read.

We had no shower and the grimy bathtub was rarely used, except by me. I don't ever remember my dad or brother taking a bath which, when I think of it now, is pretty bizarre. I didn't like taking baths much myself, since the bathroom door, like all the doors in the house, had no knob or lock. I just tried to move quickly and splash around enough to get clean, and then get out.

Giant dust balls, mounds of cat hair, crusty cat barf, desiccated dead mice, orange peels and dried macaroni were all things that lived under the couch. We didn't have a vacuum and the broom languished in a kitchen closet, draped in cobwebs.

My bedroom upstairs was a relative oasis of clean compared to the rest of the filth and decay. It was where I went to breathe, read, write and be alone, and usually, no one bothered me there.

It was painted half pink and half dark brown. I didn't know the story then, and I always wondered about the room's strange color scheme, but later on I was told that in the 1950s, when my older sister, Nora, was in the same room, Nora and Mom painted the pink room half brown.

The way she tells it, my sister had a "brown boyfriend," and when my dad forbade her to see her boyfriend anymore, she was heartbroken. Mom did the only thing she could do at the time to show solidarity with her daughter, by helping Nora roll on a coat of brown paint over the pink. That would have to do.

The pink-and-brown room was messy, but not dirty like the rest of the house. I did have cats sleeping in every nook and many stuffed animals, but I tried to make my room a sanctuary, where I could pretend to be far, far away.

I tied sheets together and hid them under my bed, for a quick escape out the window if I had to. Somehow, it was a solace to me, knowing I could one day leave, though when I actually did years later, I walked out through the front door.

It was all pretty messy, yes. Obviously it had to be that way, because it was that way. And though most things are not messy anymore for me, I still don't mind the messy parts in my life – a bit of chaos, a touch of something unexpected, an experience that may even seem like a mistake, when it's really what's needed to learn the next part.

God bless this mess.

☯

. . . . . WILL AND FORCE . . . . .

For much of my life I have used willpower to hold myself up and help me feel protected when I'm afraid. Even though I've made a habit of armoring myself and erecting whatever defense I think I need at the time, my wall of will has been feeling unnatural and contrived to me for some time now. Will has been feeling more like force.

This will, drawn up from some visceral place, has also compelled me to put my head down, crashing through whatever is in the way of what I want. Sure, sometimes we need to assert and stand up for ourselves, but there is a line that can be crossed when the assertion to exist becomes power over another.

And what about when exploitation and violence are daily occurrences? Is force always necessary when we feel we have to protect ourselves? Just what is the difference between will and force?

In lots of ways, my willfulness has been how I've survived and I'm grateful that I've had enough willpower to keep going when life's been tough. But useful as it has been, time has shown me that relying on will to propel me through life is a type of inner aggression, a refusal to accept this moment, which tenses and hardens important vulnerabilities.

Chinese medicine teaches that will comes from what's called "primordial qi" (pronounced chee), inherited from our parents and stored in the kidneys. The kidneys also house our adrenal glands, in whose cortex the hormones of "fight or flight" are produced, providing the will to run or fight what threatens us. And atop the same organs which produce the piss that's scared out of us are the glands, giving us the guts to run or fight for our lives.

I have depended on will to save me, so when I take time to sit still and be quiet, I am aware but suspicious of the subtle leaning from my dominant right side, the precursor of my nervous system's readying to do something, anything. It's not really a physical leaning, though in day-to-day activity, I notice how I inwardly twist, almost in anticipation of action, beginning with the right side of my body. Why, when there is nothing to hurt me right now, does my body insist on preparing for danger?

My left, analytical, task-oriented brain (which by the way controls the right side of my body) is accustomed to being in command of all I do. But the simple act of sitting and doing nothing makes my entire right hemisphere relax after a while. Habitual Yang dominance gives way to the receptivity of Yin, and my nervous system starts to regain a sense of choice, rather than being locked in a repetitive pattern.

For once, left brain and right side are the observed, rather than the observer, receptive and patiently allowing whatever may unfold as Yang gets a chance to exhale.

Like anything, the more we notice it, the more we notice it. And so that is my commitment, to allow will when it surfaces and to be aware if it becomes forceful to me or anyone else.

After all these years, I think I'm starting to know the difference.

. . . .

My Other Brother

My brother David wasn't around by the time I was born. He was eighteen years older than me, and from the time he was sixteen, my brother was in jail and he would be in jail for most of his life. I don't know what David did, but from a young age I'd hear that he was someone who "couldn't stay out of trouble." That's what my dad would say about him.

David was very angry, that was for sure. I remember not seeing him for years at a time, then our front door would suddenly get busted down and he'd storm in and yell at my dad. My brother, Michael, and I would sit silently, hoping our big brother wouldn't notice us on the couch. Often though, in a fit of rage and exasperation, usually because my dad wouldn't give him money, my brother would pick me up, then seeing the terror

Brother David at age 18 and me at six months

in my dad's eyes, threaten to throw me through the window if he didn't get what he was demanding.

The scene would usually end with my dad pulling twenty dollars out of his wallet, which was money we couldn't afford. Then David would leave, most often with these parting words to my father: "I'm going to piss on your grave."

Years later when I was a paramedic working the streets of downtown Vancouver, I saw my brother, high on something, filthy and lying on the curb with another guy, eating sardines out of a can with dirty fingers, laughing. I looked away, not knowing what else to do with my fear and disgust. I was just happy he didn't see me or recognize me as his little sister.

My brother David was part of my nightmares for many years. I feared him finding me wherever I was, bashing through my door and threatening whatever I held dear. When at age fifty-two, he finally died from a hard life of drugs and booze, I didn't go to his funeral. I was just relieved that he was gone.

It's been nineteen years since David died and now I finally have empathy for him. I'm curious about the life of a young man who looked like James Dean and had so much of his life stolen from him in prison.

I have a photo of my brother holding me high in the air when I was a tiny baby. Did he love his little sister? Mom loved David. He would always be her baby boy, and just about the only time I'd see her cry was when she talked about him.

What turns a person mean? What happened to my brother? Did he suffer sexual abuse from our father like my brother Michael did? I can guess, but I may never know for sure.

May your soul rest in peace, my Brother.

—— DEFENSE IS OFFENSE ——

It can be overt and easy to spot, or defense can be very subtle, barely noticeable unless we're trying to notice it. And what's wrong with defense, anyhow? Isn't it acceptable, even smart, to have defenses in place for when we feel threatened? Defensiveness can be a totally rational response to fear, but can it become habitual to put up protection, even when it might not be needed?

Is our defensiveness as individuals, as a society, as a world consciousness, part of what is making us crazy? Has our defensive posturing, defensive thinking, become a habit that's actually more like the aggression we think we're defending against? And can this be damaging to our psyche, no matter how justified we feel in our defense?

I recognize that as a straight, white person in a mostly straight, white society, it is easier for me to not be discriminated against or under attack, and so I can walk around with the luxury of not feeling like I have to be on the defense much of the time. And even though I grew up with some adversity and challenges, I am under no illusion that my struggles are nearly as profound or ongoing as what many other people live through daily. And I'm also aware that whatever struggles I've experienced can be used to inform me how to be a more effective advocate and ally.

Defensiveness has been a way of life for me. I have been too defensive to even know I was being defensive. So when I began to see how scared and protective I was, I started taking time every morning to sit quietly and notice my breath, and it's here I get to see the large and small ways I erect defenses.

It might start as a thought about the day ahead. My jaw tightens, my hands grip, my breathing and heart rate quicken, my head moves forward to prepare me for the unknown. Even in this relative state of relaxation, I can feel like a coiled spring. Yet receptivity is also present, as the small awareness of my own defense in action. I am that, too. Just noticing this is enough for me today.

My Sister in California

She's nineteen years older than me, from the same two
parents. I have a vague memory of seeing her when I was three or
so, just before my parents split, I think, then once more when I was
maybe seven, when she came to visit. I remember her crying in our
living room, talking to my dad and then leaving for her new life in
California, crying some more on her way out. I don't know what they
were talking about, but I didn't see her again till I was thirteen and
homeless, when I showed up in her life in Santa Barbara.

My sister was married and
they had a big adobe house on
the hill. It had a grand piano
in the living room, gleaming
hardwood floors and, my
favorite part, a sunny
courtyard off the kitchen. I
had my own room to stay
in. I'd never seen anything
so beautiful, so clean, with a
private bathroom, decorated
with bright Mexican tiles.
I felt like I'd stepped into
a dream. This was so
different from the filthy
house I grew up in and certainly

Me at 13 years old

different from the past few months of my life on the street. I kind
of just landed there all of a sudden. My sister didn't know me, didn't
have children of her own, and I wasn't sure if her husband was keen on
me being there.

I hadn't brought anything with me, because I didn't have anything.
I wore a pair of not-so-clean underwear, jeans and a T-shirt, and some

flip-flops, so my sister saw it as her duty to take me shopping every day. She'd brush my hair, put makeup on me, spray me with perfume and off we'd go to the department stores, where anything I hesitantly admired was magically mine.

We made a day trip to Los Angeles, so my sister could show me where she'd worked at NBC Studios, where we walked around there a bit, passing someone that I'm pretty sure was Johnny Carson, who laughed when he saw my "Hollywood Hills" t-shirt and said, "Hey! Are those the Hollywood Hills?" I smiled, but wanted to disappear right then.

Next we went for a stroll on Hollywood Boulevard to see the stars on the sidewalk. At one point when we were walking, she pulled me over to the side.

"What are you doing?" she demanded.

"What? I'm not doing anything."

1990 with Mom and Nora

"Yes you are! You are looking in each person's eyes as we walk past them. Don't you know that men take that as a challenge? You can't do that!"

I was stunned. Looking in the eyes of people was how I learned if I could trust them, if I was safe or not. I felt defensive and overwhelmed walking in this unfamiliar aggressive place full of strange people. I was scared, so my survival mechanism had kicked in and I was checking everyone out to see if they were friend or foe.

I stayed for a week or two in that bubble of unreality in Santa Barbara. I thought maybe I'd be staying there for good. No one asked me much about myself or where I would go when I went back, so after a few days I thought I'd just be sort of adopted and that this would be my new home. But it wasn't my new home. She drove me to the airport, where we both cried and waved goodbye.

I came to visit Nora every so often, but for years I was bitter and resentful that she hadn't taken me in to live with her when I was a teen. My sister and I argued a lot on the phone and whenever we'd see each other. I was hostile, mean and had a lot of what I thought were good reasons to keep her at arm's length and on my shit list. She suffered from my treatment of her, and I made her wear the guilt of "abandoning" me when she had so much. I suffered, too. My bitterness hurt us both.

Hearing about how life was for her growing up in our family, I know that it was very difficult for my sister. She tells me how our parents fought violently, with "Mom running screaming out of the house in her half-slip and bra so all the neighbors knew it was a madhouse."

Nora told me how she'd cower under the bathroom sink as our father punched and kicked, calling her names. At age sixteen she finally left and stayed at her friend's family's home a few blocks away, then moved to California a few years later to get as far away as possible.

So growing up for her was no picnic either.

Over the years I've traded the bitterness for learning how to forgive, starting with myself, continuing on to working on healing my relationship with my sister. Now we talk on the phone often and see each other whenever we can. It's not always easy, but we both keep on loving one another, wanting to make up for the years of lost time. Nora never had children of her own and so she dotes on me, sending gifts and cards to show me that I'm important to her. I feel blessed to have her in my life.

Grandma

My grandmother looked like the perfect little old lady. She had soft, milky skin and long white hair that I'd watch her patiently brush at night when we'd stay at her house. We'd go over there most Sundays for dinner and watch *The Ed Sullivan Show* on the old black-and-white TV.

I always felt like I'd better be on my best behavior there, not that anyone told me to be "good," but when we were at Grandma's, I got the same feeling at her house as I did at home when my dad was about to blow his top. I sensed a barely contained rage at her house, somewhere under the smell of boiled potatoes and canned ham. I just knew to tread carefully.

I didn't know it then, but Grandma did have a history of mental illness and she took it out on her children. My sister told me years later that Grandma was a "beauty" who, contrary to the norms of her generation, was not interested in marriage and was even less interested in having children. She reluctantly got married and proceeded to have four children who were terrorized by her fits of rage.

My dad told me casually one day when I was ten, just after Grandma died, "She chased us around the table with a butcher knife and my dad would have to tie her up in the basement for hours until she calmed down." I was getting great insight into my father's childhood and why at age fifteen he "hopped the freights" to Alberta to get away.

The history of how my dad grew up illustrates how his violence, his helplessness, his twisted sense of right and wrong, was all bound up in a childhood of terror and loss. My father abused his children like he was abused. He beat them and sexually tormented them because of what he might have experienced at home, where he should have felt safe and loved.

Understanding how the roots of my dad's pain caused him to hurt others is not a way to minimize or invalidate what he did. My

Grandma must have suffered, too, when she was a child, to carry such destructive toxic anger.

I will probably never know what Grandma's young life was like, but allowing myself to see hers and my dad's lives clearly, helps me to forgive and learn how not to be. My family has taught me a lot about how not to be, and that is a blessing.

WHY ZEBRAS
—— DON'T GET ULCERS ——

The title of Robert Sapolsky's book tells us something about how the wild animal kingdom effectively copes with stress, while we as humans generally don't cope well at all.

A hungry lion chases a juicy-looking zebra grazing on the savanna. The zebra's nervous system response of fight or flight kicks in and the zebra runs like mad, evading the lion. Then, once it's safe, the grazing resumes and all is well. The zebra discharges stress hormones from its nervous system by running, and therefore has no elevated blood cortisol that can cause stress-related diseases like ulcers.

So what can we learn from how the zebra lives? Stress-related autoimmune diseases like lupus, MS, psoriasis, Crohn's disease and type 2 diabetes are on the rise, all directly related to how much stress we carry and how we fail to discharge that stress. Instead, we internalize it and it is making us ill.

To change anything, we must become aware of what it is we are doing to help create the problem. Awareness, as usual, is the first place to go. Notice what your mind, body and emotions are doing. Are you holding your breath? Just notice, and as quantum physics has shown, our mere observation of something has the power to alter it.

Wild Child

My brother Michael and I dressed funny, with old and dirty hand-me-downs that didn't get washed often, and our family was just known for being strange and different. When I got teased at school I tried to rise above it and not let it get me down. My brother had a harder time, eventually just withdrawing more and more. He never had any friends, except me.

After school Michael and I walked home together across a big playing field. Kids would chase us, throw things, call us names, and the only time I really fought back was when they'd gang up on my brother.

Michael was sickly, thin, and allergic to peanuts, which caused him to be weak and phlegmy from his frequent asthma attacks. When he was ten my dad thought it would be a good idea to "toughen him up" by putting Michael on the football team. I was a tiny junior cheerleader, wearing a red sweater and white skirt, which was actually just a shortened ladies' slip from Goodwill. Unfortunately, football was not his sport and the same bullies from school now had free license to pummel him and knock him down whenever they could.

One day, sitting on the sidelines watching Michael get beat up, I couldn't stand it anymore, so I walked onto the field in the middle of the game, kicked one of the players in the shin, and yelled at them all to "Just leave him alone!" Then I took Michael's hand and walked home with him. My dad saw his bloodied nose and mud-caked uniform, and that was the last football game Michael had to play. I quit my stint as a cheerleader in solidarity with my brother.

I somehow became popular in grade three and my friends would fight over who got to play with me after school. I think it was because coming to our house meant you could run around, yell and scream, and not have anyone tell you to be quiet. Once it was decided who was my pick, we'd choose whose house to go to. Our house was close to the school, so we'd go there most often to play with our many cats, climb trees and just cut loose before my dad came home.

When we'd go to my friends' houses, we didn't have as much fun, because there were adults around and rules to follow, and you had to say, "May I be excused?" before you left the dinner table. During dinner at our house, Michael and I had food fights with our mashed potatoes, snorted milk through our noses, and the cats sat on the table while we ate, watching *Gilligan's Island*.

My next-door neighbor friend Johnny and I rode our bikes to the golf course and through culverts there, stopping to eat a can of beans and swim in the streams. We watched *The Great Escape* on TV and decided to dig a tunnel in the backyard, which we got quite a lot done on before my dad put a stop to it. We used to climb a giant cottonwood tree in the backyard and hide there till after dark, listening to our parents calling us to come in. Sometimes I think we could have just stayed there among the sweet-smelling leaves, with the birds perched at eye level.

I was a wild child, semi-feral and happiest when I could do what I pleased and get dirty doing it. My favorite times were lying in the grass, watching insects traveling their tiny worlds, oblivious to mine. I admired my cats and the freedom they had, so I'd go climbing through fences and under things, as I tried my best to follow them on their neighborhood journeys.

I remember these times of adventure and discovery even more vividly than when I was confused and hurt. Some green, silent part of those years growing up stays with me still…

Sundays

I have a lot of harsh, brutal memories of being young, and some memories that will be the last flashes I see when I die because they are so beautiful. The more I write, the more the harsh and beautiful become … integrated, part of the whole, not good or bad, just life …

On Sundays after church we'd often head to one of my dad's favorite places, Queen Elizabeth Park, the old granite quarry that was turned into a spectacular botanical garden.

There is an enormous dome-shaped conservatory at the top of the hill, full of tropical plants and birds. It was a great place to spend a chilly wet day and when you closed your eyes you felt like you were in paradise. Fountains beside the conservatory fed into streams running all the way down in different directions into ponds, creating a kid's fantasy playground.

My brother Michael, my Dad and me

On cold winter Sunday afternoons my dad would take me there so I could skate on the ponds. I had a pair of boy's hockey skates, the only ones we could find at Goodwill that fit. Seeing my disappointment, my dad painted on a temporary coat of shoe whitener to make them look like the Ice-Capades skates I dreamed of. Usually it was just the two of us there and my dad would sit in the car listening to the radio, or taking a snooze, while I became Snow White, practicing my pirouettes on the sparkling ice.

On sunny Sunday afternoons we'd go straight from church to Queen E (I always thought it was *Queeny*) Park to play around in the streams making dams. We'd giggle watching my dad roll up his pant legs and take off his shoes. He'd make funny, tortured faces when his big white feet slipped into the water, making us laugh even more.

He'd show us how to scoop up mud, sticks, rocks and anything that would create a dam to hold back the water. All the kids, even kids we didn't know who were there with their own parents, would join in, squealing, laughing and just having fun.

"Tear down the wall!" my dad would call out, and we'd all start pulling at the sticks and mud till a torrent poured forth. I usually liked to get in the water's path, pretending to be carried away in the rush of water.

"Help! Help! I'm drowning in the rapids!" I'd scream, rolling in the muddy water in my Sunday best. I think that was my favorite part, being allowed to get filthy and wet, without anyone disapproving of me or telling me what to do.

The feeling of freedom and peace would stay with me for a long time … a warm open space in my chest.

We'd spend the whole day there. Time didn't exist. The ice cream truck drove by and we all got popsicles. Blue- and orange-lipped kids, blissfully silent on the drive home, fingertips and toes all wrinkled and pruny, we were too tired for supper.

We slept like dogs.

I think these were some of my dad's most precious times with us, too, and maybe they were like good memories he'd shared with his father. I hope so.

I can see him there right now, smiling, wanting us to be happy, trying to be a good father … And in a lot of ways, he was.

HEALTH AND
····· ILLNESS DEFERRED ·····

When we become ill, we are often surprised that one day we feel "fine" and the next day here we are feeling unwell or getting a diagnosis of illness from the doctor. We might even feel a sense of betrayal when our bodies don't cooperate by responding how we'd like them to. Illness doesn't just happen, though — we become ill from the impact of all things in our lives, including physical causes like germs and other pathogens, as well as emotional events and patterns, day-to-day stress, eating habits, lifestyle habits and genetic predispositions.

When I speak to my patients about their conditions, I like to make the analogy of a person going for a five-mile run. If they run five miles once every six months, there will be little to no impact on their health. If the same person runs half a mile every day, there will be a big positive impact on their health. Our health or illness depends on the habits we cultivate and commit to every day. If we smoke every day, eat junk food every day, don't take time for stillness, don't move our bodies in some form of exercise, we will reap the consequences of those choices.

It's difficult in our society of instant gratification to trust the process of living each day as a foundation for the next. There are no guarantees and always exceptions to the rule, but nature teaches best with her consistent patterns, showing how one season affects the following seasons.

A very wet, snowy winter creates a storehouse of moisture to regulate the heat of summer by melting and flowing into streams and groundwater to make plants grow, further protecting the earth with moisture. In a dry winter season there are not enough reserves of moisture stored. Excess heat turns to consuming fire. Balance is lost.

With a little persistence, we can change our diet and cut out the daily soft drinks and in time we lose weight and have more energy to move and feel better. Consistency and commitment are how we show we care, in this case, about ourselves.

We can learn at any stage of life and any stage of illness to start small, daily preparation for more fertile, healthy conditions in our bodies, minds and spirits. The first place to start is with the next breath we take. We can be aware, take a deeper and slower breath next time, then make a point of taking of ten slow, deep breaths every night before bed. Small things make the biggest difference when we make them a habit.

The journey of a thousand miles begins with a single step. —Lao Tzu

. . . .

Cats

There is a house in most neighborhoods full of crazy people, or at least one crazy cat lady, and a lot of cats. That was our house. As my animal stories often begin, there was one, and then there were many…

We had one cat named Kitty. Kitty was a big orange long-haired tomcat who scratched and bit, but would let me pick him up and take him to bed with me at night. He put up with me cuddling him and petting him, like good cats will do with their human children.

I loved Kitty so much that when we'd go on a car vacation, driving to BC's interior or across the line into the U.S., Kitty came along, bundled up with me in the back seat on blankets and pillows. He was usually very good and Kitty would come back if he wandered off when we stopped somewhere. Even when we were camping, Kitty slept in the tent on top of my sleeping bag.

We were camping near Nelson, BC, one night, getting in after dark to set up. I quickly fell asleep with Kitty on my chest, but in the night he must have wandered out of the tent, because in the morning he was gone. We looked and looked but couldn't find him anywhere. We gave the campground people our phone number in case they saw Kitty, but they never called.

I cried all the way home, and for weeks I'd keep thinking I saw Kitty, imagining he'd done like Lassie and had walked back to me across the mountains. A couple of months later my dad came home from his job driving cab with a mewing kitten in each pocket of his sport coat. Of course I was in love, and those were my new kitties to mend my broken heart.

Cats are like rabbits. They breed whenever possible, so within a few months we had several more kitties. Kids don't know any better. It would have been good if my dad had been more responsible and had gotten the cats fixed before they multiplied, but that wasn't the case. Our little cat farm kept growing.

Kitties were everywhere. At least six or seven slept on my bed at night, or in my open dresser drawers, where they had their kittens sometimes, too. Every piece of clothing I had was covered in cat fur and, worse still, cat pee, which you stop noticing after a while if it's in your house, though other people do still notice. My little friends would come over after school to play and their mothers would complain that when they came home they smelled like cat pee. Not much I could do about it.

I started life as a crazy cat child and I am well on my way to being a crazy cat lady, but I only have one cat right now. She is a darling rescue cat named Kitty. Some things never change. Most of my cats have been named Kitty, with the exception of those who had names when I got them: Sid, the unforgettable orange tabby who lived on the boat with me; Samantha, the rotund and not-so-cuddly Russian blue; Barnaby and Charlie, who came to me in a wicker basket from England; and my dear, favorite cat of all, the tiny Siamese Baby Kitty, God rest her sweet soul.

Thinking of all this now, it feels like there's just something missing from my life; I think I need a few more cats ...

Trust

Not everyone knows how it feels to trust. It takes the experience of trust and the memory of it to recognize the feeling when it comes again. I know how it feels to trust now, but for much of my life I could not imagine trusting anyone.

When my mom fled the violence of our home, my brother and I were very young. I can only imagine how hard it was for her to leave us behind and I understand why she came back early in the morning, months later, to take us with her. My dad was at work. When he came home, we were gone.

I remember the bus ride to the other side of town. I was tightly clutched on her lap; the three of us sat in stunned silence, too afraid to say anything. We got off the bus and it was raining hard as we walked up the long hill to her place. I remember feeling so happy being with Mom again, so safe, cuddled in her perfume-smelling blankets, eating the oranges she'd peel for us. I never wanted to be anywhere else.

We had a lot of fun in that dark little flat. There was a purple blanket Michael would put on his head, pretending to be our big sister, Nora, with her long dark hair, and he chased me around and made me laugh. We tried to be quiet, just like she told us, so the landlady upstairs wouldn't complain. One rule Mom was very strict about was that we were never, ever to play in the front yard of the house. We didn't know the reason, but we tried to do as she asked. It seemed important.

It was a bright autumn day as we ran in the yard playing tag. The sun was warm and sweet-smelling leaves crunched underfoot. Michael chased me around the side and front of the house as I laughed gleefully. Then he stopped. There at the top of the street was my dad, standing by his car, waving and crouching down with his arms outstretched to his two children, whom he'd not seen in weeks.

I froze. Michael started running towards our dad. My legs felt stuck to the ground and my chest felt hollow. Michael grabbed my hand and pulled me up the street with him, where we were scooped into my dad's arms and into the car.

It'd be nine years till I got to see our mother again.

It was an impossible decision for a child to make. For years I believed I'd done the wrong thing by leaving Mom that day. I believed I didn't know how to make a good decision. I lost trust in myself.

It's taken half a lifetime to realize how what happened so long ago impacted me and where my beliefs have come from. I know now that I did the only thing a three-year-old could have done. I trusted my brother, took his hand, and followed him.

Healing has happened for me over time as I have had help to deconstruct my belief that I was not capable of making a good decision. I had to go back to the specific time when I disconnected with myself in order to reconnect with who I am.

Trust is precious, and never so precious as when it is lost and found again.

——— AMAZING GRACE ———

We are amazed by grace because we so often don't leave room for it in our lives. Grace floats into the spaces between our doubts and pain. Prayer invites grace when we surrender our idea of what we think is right or best, surrendering to what's beyond our control. We are amazed that even without our struggles to make things how we want them, grace finds the most elegant way to teach us what we're here to learn. We do not need to deserve grace, because it does not recognize such a thing. Like air, grace is available for everyone, always.

I get in the way of acceptance of this moment, which is where grace resides. My work is to allow the power of grace to infuse what I do in life by not fighting things so much. Instead, may I be loving and inviting, not pushing, demanding, grasping or raging in my ignorance of what grace is quietly accomplishing. This is my prayer.

Doors

My brother Michael and I were the second "generation" of kids raised in the old veteran-style home in South East Vancouver. My sister and oldest brother David were raised in the same house almost twenty years earlier. There were about five different styles of homes, all of which were made available as cheap housing for veterans when their service was done. Ours was the steep-roofed green one in the middle of a crescent, facing south towards Richmond. We had a red front door.

The front door and all the doors in the house were strangely broken. The front door frame was cracked, from all the times my oldest brother, David, would kick it down in a rage, fresh out of jail and demanding money from my dad, splintering red-painted chips of wood over the floor, like little shards of blood.

Months would go by with the damaged door half off its hinges so it couldn't be closed all the way, then when it rained a lot, the wood swelled and the door could barely open. If it got really bad, my dad would get a hammer and some nails and patch it together till the next time my brother David came around, because there always was a next time.

The back door from the kitchen went onto a porch where the

clothesline was attached. I loved standing on a stool and pegging one of my green plastic army men to it, pulling the line and sending him all the way to the post at other side of the yard, like he was flying. I tried a couple of times to hold onto the line myself and fly like my army man, but both times I fell and my dad got mad.

One time I was in and out of the house playing with the clothesline and my dad accidentally shut my finger in the door, crushing the tip of the middle finger of my left hand. I think it might have broken the finger and my dad looked like he felt so bad that I tried not to cry, but it really hurt. That finger has always been bent and the nail still grows funny.

None of the doors on the inside of the house had door knobs. Instead, there was only a hole where the knob had been. It wasn't so bad for some of the closets because you could just find an old sock and jam it in to make it stay shut, but a sock didn't help if you wanted the privacy of a securely shut door.

My bedroom had no knob, so I could never really shut the door tight. My brother Michael loved scaring me by sneaking up so I couldn't hear him and kicking the door in, commando style, just like big brother David would do…And my dad would often burst into my room, too, and sit on the bed, especially when I had friends staying the night. I'd freeze and feel confused and embarrassed. I was always relieved when he'd stand up and leave.

What really bothered me was that there was no way of securing the bathroom door. There was a sock tied through the hole where the latch would have been, for ease of pulling it closed, but then you had to find a way to plug the hole where the knob was, so no one could look in. I tried lots of things, like socks or dishrags, which my brother would either pull out or push through, just for the hell of it.

I think it was his way of acting out how his own boundaries were being trampled on with the sexual abuse he suffered. Neither of us ever felt safe.

My bedroom had an attic door about four feet high, leading to a long, narrow room along the eaves of the house. It was the only door in the house with a knob, so it was my favorite door. I liked going in there, where it was dark and I could hear the rain hitting the roof. Birds tweeted in the trees outside, which brushed against the house; neighbors talked in their yards, cars drove by, lawnmowers droned and, at the same time, I could hear the inside sounds of the TV downstairs, the fridge opening and closing, my dad in the kitchen. Shutting the attic door tightly behind me felt luxurious and relaxing, like I was somewhere else.

Kids find ways to cope in all different circumstances and my way was to try to find something in my immediate environment to tune in to. Even now, though, it may be old stuff, but I do sleep more soundly when the bedroom door is securely shut. It just feels better to me.

Triggers and ── Healing Traumas ──

The term "triggered" describes how something happening in the present moment can bring up emotions from a similar time in the past. Not just emotions arise, but bodily sensations connected to stimulation of the nervous system become engaged and suddenly we feel as if we are re-experiencing past stress.

When we are triggered we may experience being frightened, anxious, confused, angry, sad, or many other feelings. Heart palpitations, sweating, dry mouth and digestive irritation are just some of the physical sensations that come with sympathetic nervous system upregulation, caused by stress, resulting in decisions which might not be in our best interest, or we may even strike out at others, verbally or physically.

Certain things can cause a pattern of stress response to become triggered and whether or not we become stressed can also depend on factors like whether we have eaten, rested well, already had a lot of stress that particular day, or are coming down with a cold or flu. The quality of our past interactions with people also affects our responses, as do many other ways we are influenced personally by our environment. All these things impact the way we perceive stimuli and how we interpret what we see, hear, smell and, therefore, think and feel.

The good news is that getting into the habit of checking in, being curious and standing back a bit from responses, makes space for change to happen. Our nervous systems need a little room in order to become less brittle and more elastic, and this in turn restores the ability to choose responses, rather than simply falling into the over-stimulated, knee-jerk response of a burned-out nervous system.

I got triggered today. I was walking alone in a bleak industrial area, it was getting dark, I didn't know where the bus stop was and I thought I was lost. I know it may sound like nothing, but I found my mind and emotions going back to times many years ago, when I would be alone, scared, on the street when it was dark, and I didn't know where to go. So that is what started coming up for me. I was being triggered.

I noticed what was going on in my mind and emotions, then I tried to touch in with myself. I stopped walking, took a deep breath, felt my feet on the ground, got my wooly hat out of my bag, put it on and kept walking till things started looking familiar. I went into a store to get warm and called my husband to hear a friendly voice. He was so kind, he drove over and picked me up, but not because I was panicked. I never got to that point.

I consider myself a strong, resilient person. I have been through a lot, yet, I am only human and I intend to keep healing the trauma in my life by giving my loving attention to those times I am scared or confused. When I notice strong feelings coming up, I try to remember to find some objectivity between my thoughts and emotions. That way my responses can come from being conscious *and aware to what is actually happening, rather than my responses coming from traumatic memories.*

Contrary to what we often say or think, people do not "make us feel" one way or another. If we believe "people make us feel," we are abdicating our ability to choose our responses and heal our trauma. We get triggered because of our unhealed past experiences. Noticing triggers and healing our trauma takes some time, patience, gentleness and, mostly, practice.

And we're all worth it.

The Backyard

I liked to sit on the porch and watch my dad mow the lawn in our backyard. He'd carefully push the mower down each row, overlapping the wheels on the next turn so it was perfect. He looked content and satisfied, doing this simple task, and in those moments when I'd see his face all calm and serene, he seemed to be at peace and it made me feel good.

When he'd pause to wipe his brow, I'd often bring my dad a glass of grape Kool-Aid so I could bask in his enjoyment of a cool drink on a hot day. "Ah, that's so good," he'd say, patting my head, smiling with a faraway look in his eyes. My heart would swell and I'd wish I could make time stand still right then, just to hold the moment forever.

My sister Nora tells me stories about when she grew up in that same house and my dad would make big bonfires in the backyard where they'd roast wieners and marshmallows. We never did that, but I like the memory anyhow and I imagine some better days there before I was born, when Mom and Nora and David were there with my dad as a family.

We got a pool from Sears one year and all the kids in our neighborhood came to swim and play, while it lasted. Near the end of that first summer, the sides split open while my friend Trudy and I were paddling around, sending us sliding and squealing in a flood of water onto the lawn.

When the weather was colder, the cats were out there with me on their rounds through the wet grass. They accepted me as one of their own and we were wild animals for our time outside, until it was time to come in to a warm house, where we were once more domestic creatures, slit-eyed on the warm chesterfield, bellies full and dreaming of our next adventures.

☯

LEARN HOW TO
····· TAKE CARE OF SELF ·····

My beautiful and wise Asian acupuncturist "Doctor Jenny" treated me every week for a year, chiding me for my delicate and rundown state of health, from so many years of ambulance work and stress.

"You are just a young woman. How do you get so tired and sick? When will you rest and eat properly?" I liked her admonitions, though. I felt mothered and she gave me clear directions: "Eat more warm food. Stop and relax when eating. Don't work too hard during periods. Sleep important. More sleep. No more stress."

I did try my best to follow Dr. Jenny's advice and I kept coming for acupuncture, taking her herbal formulas in between appointments. "This formula my father gave me when I was thirteen and started period," she told me. "Boost blood, clear stagnation, keep uterus healthy." I took that, too, and with each passing week, I felt stronger, more like the young woman I was. My outlook on life changed and I had an epiphany.

"Doctor Jenny! I have decided to quit the ambulance service and go back to school. I want to be an acupuncturist!" I said breathlessly during one of my weekly acupuncture treatments.

Doctor Jenny didn't look up as she inserted the next needle into my leg. "Good. Learn how to take care of self."

I'm still learning. It's a lifelong process. Thank you Doctor Jenny.

. . . .

Not Enough Rocks

Thinking about the house I grew up in still opens up a lot of memories for me and some of those are memories I'd rather forget.

In my favorite movie, *Forrest Gump*, there is a scene where Forrest and Jenny are walking and they come across the small deserted home where she grew up. She throws one of her shoes, and then the other, before she begins picking up rocks from the dusty road to hurl at the house, breaking some windows before she drops sobbing to the ground. Without understanding, Forrest sees that she is upset and we hear his voice saying, "Sometimes there just aren't enough rocks."

Forrest recollects childhood memories with Jenny, saying how her father was "A very loving man. He was always kissing and touching her and her sisters"…Then we see Forrest and Jenny as children, running wildly through the cornfield, with her father yelling angrily behind. Just from these scenes, we are able to understand what it was like to be Jenny growing up in that house. The scene always gives me goosebumps and makes me cry. I would have stood there and thrown those rocks with her. Forrest did even better when he had the place bulldozed.

My fourth grade teacher, Mrs. Preston, moved into the house next door to us. I had just finished a year with her and she was always so kind and doting to me, patting me on the head and telling me my hair was nice, which I know it wasn't. I think she just felt maternal and protective towards me because she didn't have children of her own. I was thrilled that my pretty and sweet teacher would be our new neighbor, though I'm not sure she was as thrilled to be living so close to our madhouse and it must have been hard for her to try to keep a professional distance, while still caring about the welfare of the kids living next door.

My brother Michael and me in front of the house

It was summer and we were out of school. My dad was at work driving cab and as usual my brother and I were fighting. It didn't take much to set him off because he had so much pent up rage from being sexually abused by our dad. I don't even remember why it started, but Michael started hitting me and chased me upstairs to my bedroom, where he pushed me on the bed and sat on my chest punching and punching me in the face.

Usually I'd fight back while I could, but he was bigger, four years older, and I was starting to give up. My nose was bleeding and as he kept punching I opened my eyes and saw that my window was open on the side of the house next to Mrs. Preston's. Feeling desperate, I let out the most blood curdling scream I could muster, hoping that somehow she would hear me.

"Rebekah? Is that you? Are you alright?" she asked up at the window. The punching magically stopped and Michael froze.

"Yes, I'm fine. Thank you Mrs. Preston!" I sang down to her. "I just saw a mouse and got scared."

"Okay dear. Let me know if you ever need anything. I'm here."

"Thank you. I will."

It bought me some time. And not only did I get away from him that day, but I got beat up way less often from then on, thanks to Mrs. Preston. My brother knew I had an ally.

When I went back to look at that old house decades later, it had been bulldozed and another new one was built in its place. When I could have, I wish I'd done what Jenny did, but there'd never have been enough rocks…

Forgiveness
—— is Forgetting ——

Someone once said to me, "Forgiveness is forgetting." I thought about it for a long time, not really agreeing with the statement. How could I "forget" whatever I was hurt or angry about and how was that connected to forgiveness? Was it even possible not to remember something I felt had wounded me? Time heals all things, right? Time goes by and new things happen and one day the pain, anger and hurt in the forefront of our minds begins to fade away…or does it?

I held on to the pain of losing my mom early in life, for a really long time. I know I was holding on because strong emotion was right at the surface if I started thinking about her leaving my brother and me behind. I'd begin constructing all the ways she was wrong and ruined my life. It was easier to be angry than to be deeply sad.

Letting myself feel the deep sadness I'd never expressed just scared me. Sadness was a familiar bottomless pit, a dark abyss I never wanted to be anywhere near again. So I raged instead, acted out instead – drinking, doing drugs, seeing who could love me and who would leave me. They always left; I'd make sure of that.

Healing work, lots of help, humility and, yes, time showed me how I could feel pain and not be swallowed by it. I can remember what caused my painful feelings, but now I most often forget to act on the impulse to be angry about my life.

I actually have learned to forgive, through integrating experiences, and now I even forget to be who I once was. I haven't mastered the art of forgiveness, but it's easier when I allow what has happened in my life to be part of who I am. This is integration.

Monica

Because I was "raised by wolves" in a crazy house with my dad, brother and about twenty flea-bitten cats, I was usually the kid parents cast a wary eye on when their children became friends with me. They had to watch that I wasn't a bad influence on their sweet little darlings, with their perfect pigtails and white knee-high socks.

My friend Monica's parents always watched carefully while we gleefully ran through sprinklers on their front lawn, though I never understood why Monica wasn't allowed to play at my house, where no one really cared what you did.

Monica came over after school one day anyhow, though, and I convinced her to "wax the floor" with me. Finding a tin of ancient floor wax in the cupboard under the sink, we threw huge globs of it on our filthy kitchen floor, littered with hair, cat crunchies, dried bits of food. "Watch Monica! We can skate around. Take off your shoes and play with me!"

We had loads of fun, doing "Ice Capades" stunts to my loud

humming of circus tunes, until my dad got home from work, exhausted and yelling at us to "Stop that right now!" which sent me defiantly rolling on the sticky floor with laughter and a terrified Monica running all the way home in her stocking feet, covered in wax.

One weekend I found an interesting looking book at a garage sale and took it home. The title, *Xaviera Goes Wild*, intrigued me and as I read it I just knew my friend Monica, who loved anything body related, like smelly farts and burps, would just love this!

Monica's strict German parents enrolled her in ballet, gymnastics, piano and, of course, German lessons, believing their darling daughter should have only the best in life and I'm sure they wanted to keep her out of trouble by making sure she was always occupied with edifying activities and in only the finest company.

I think Monica admired me for the absolute freedom I enjoyed, even if that freedom was actually neglect of some of my basic needs. For Monica, I imagine I was a sort of role model for how she really would like to have lived as a kid. We'd known one another since preschool and were as inseparable as two girls could be during our elementary school years, till I brought *Xaviera Goes Wild* over to her house one day after school.

We giggled and squirmed, reading the hard-core porn adventures of Xaviera, the Happy Hooker, screwing everything and everyone that walked, with her colorful descriptions of sex with men, women, animals and all kinds of inanimate objects. "It makes me feel funny down there," squealed Monica, as we hid under her European down quilt.

"I know! Me too!" I squealed, rolling around on the floor.

We were having such fun, until her mother came in to see what all the noise was about. "What's this?" she demanded, grabbing the book from my hand. Scowling and pointing at me, with one of the meanest faces I've ever seen, Monica's mom said, "Now you go home right now and don't you ever come back here!"

I stood up, ready to laugh, since that's what usually disarmed my dad when he was angry, but she slapped me hard on the bum, grabbed my arm and shoved me out the front door. The last thing

I saw was poor Monica's pale, twisted face, before I trudged home across the playing fields, shocked and sick to my stomach.

The next day at school Monica told me her dad had come home and gave her a hard spanking for her reckless behavior with "that bad friend of yours." The worst part was, she told me, sobbing, "I'm not ever allowed to play with you again. They said you can't come over again, ever. I don't know what to do. How can we possibly survive?" she said dramatically.

"I don't know," I muttered. "I feel like puking."

Losing Monica as an after-school playmate broke both our hearts. We were only eight or so and we'd been friends since we were four, but as time went by, birthdays went by without being able to attend one another's parties, and we eventually grew apart, replaced by other friends in each other's lives. Her parents got their wish to keep us separated, but they'll never know how much we both hurt. I still miss her.

I doubt I could track down Monica now. Who knows where she is? If we ever did see each other again, though, I'm sure we'd laugh and cry like old times. I just know we would…

And I bet her mom kept the book. I'll bet you anything she did.

6

······ WHAT NOT TO DO ······

When we get sick or something is out of balance in life, we usually look for what we can do to make things better. So often, though, we'd be better served by looking close at what might have led to the imbalance in the first place and then work backwards from there. It's figuring out what not to do that will make the biggest difference.

There's an old joke: A man goes to his doctor and says, "Doctor, it hurts when I bend over." The doctor says, "Well, then don't bend over." Sure, it's a simplistic answer but maybe not so far off.

I saw a patient recently, a young man in his early 20s who had been diagnosed with gastritis, an inflammatory condition of the stomach. His doctor gave him an antacid medication to give his stomach "time to heal" and told him to lay off coffee. While the medication might be helpful in the short term, the advice to "lay off coffee" was even more helpful to stop the problem from recurring. What not to do is the first step.

Inflammatory conditions are just that: inflammation, heat to be specific. Heat comes from foods that are hot in nature, like hot peppers and other spices, and substances like coffee and alcohol. In East Asian medicine heat is Yang, hot and dominant, and is also produced when our bodies do not have enough time to rest. The stress of running on high speed all the time will sooner or later lead to dryness (Yin deficiency) and like a motor with no oil, it will burn up.

My advice for my young patient was to pay attention to what his body was telling him at this early stage. I told him to stop spicy food, late nights, eating on the run, and to cut out coffee and alcohol. Besides all that, at the root of his condition, stress had been burning in the background, so I advised him to do yoga or something calming to give his nervous system a break.

Like a wise person had once told me: "Eat slowly, no spicy, rest, sleep, no stress, breathe. Learn how to take care of self. Learn what not to do."

· ·

Babysitters

With Mom gone and my dad working, Michael and I had to fend for ourselves a lot. Sometimes we had babysitters and sometimes we were alone. I liked it best when we had babysitters, because there was another pair of eyes to watch over us and that way I felt safer, because then Michael was less likely to hit me.

Doris was a cool teenager who lived two doors down and she'd come over to hang out for a few hours till our dad got home from his part-time work driving cab. I liked Doris, though I'm sure I was a pest, the way I clung to her and followed her everywhere.

Doris used to brush my long hair and patiently, gently get all the tangles out while I sat on the stool in front of my Mom's old vanity with the round mirror. She'd tell me I was pretty and she'd bring lots of bobby pins and elastics over from her house, to style my hair like a movie star.

For a while a young guy from the church came to live with us and so part of earning his keep was to babysit Michael and me while my dad wasn't home. His name was Doug and my dad told us, "Doug is a Newfie," which meant that Doug was from Newfoundland, where my dad had been stationed in the air force.

Doug's broad Newfie accent made him sound like his mouth was full of marbles, which made us kids laugh rudely. Doug didn't seem to mind much. He'd surely been teased before about his funny accent, pock-marked skin and coke-bottle-thick glasses.

Doug was lots of fun and even when we stole his glasses, making him almost blind, and snuck up behind to scare him, he forgave us and was always nice, though he did move out after a couple of weeks. Can't say that I blamed him.

Sometimes there was no one to take care of us so we tagged along with our dad while he worked doing dispatch. We both loved coming to the taxi office in Richmond, playing around in the back parking lot on the stacks of tires, or finding stray kitties that I'd hide in the car and take home to add to the twenty or so we already had.

My favorite part was when my dad would make up the trunk of the car into a big bed for us to sleep in during his graveyard shifts there. The old '55 Cadillac had an enormous trunk and with layers of blankets, pillows and some kittens, it was a comfy place to curl up. It was funny that when we were there with my dad at the taxicab office, we just had fun and never fought the way we did at home.

Later on we had other babysitters, some of whom only came once and then never again. I remember how ten-year-old Michael got mad at one of them who tried to get him to stop hitting me, so he hit her, too, and that was the last we saw of her.

Our neighbor Mrs. Moir died. She was my favorite babysitter Doris' mom and not much time went by before her dad remarried a nice woman with a son named Johnny.

Johnny became my best friend and I spent lots of time over at his house with his mom, who made me toast with marmalade and let us play loudly in the backyard till it got dark. I even got to spend the night there, sleeping in a pup tent we pitched in Johnny's room, and she'd bring us sticks of beef jerky, saying, "Here's your rations soldiers. Make them last!"

I pretended that Johnny was my real brother and his Mom was my Mom, too. I actually think Johnny's mom loved me and did her best to help me feel like I had a normal, good place to come to. I will always remember that.

There are so many people I think of and I wonder where they are now, if they are okay and what happened in their lives. They may never know how much they meant to me, but I hope I meant something to them, too.

The vivid things I recall are still as fresh as the day they happened and even if not all of it was easy, I still wouldn't change a thing.

—— When We Cringe ——

It's when we say or do something that doesn't feel genuine that we cringe inside. But why does this happen? Where are we "coming from" when we behave in ways that don't feel like "who we are"?

I learned early in life that in order to survive, I had to put aside my own feelings and try to do what I thought others wanted me to do. I was trying to be safe and I didn't want to complain, so after a while this became a habit and I forgot how to stand up for myself. I believed I was keeping the peace, but I felt anything but peaceful when people were hurting me. I disconnected from my feelings and who I was.

I notice now when I am dis-connected and just trying to please. The signals come on strong and there is no denying that when I start to cringe, I know that I'm off track. So when I find myself compromising my authenticity, I stop what I am doing or saying. Sometimes it looks weird, I'm sure, but I feel honest, strong and good when I give myself another chance to sincerely try again.

Hand-me-downs

We didn't have much money and I didn't have many clothes, so a lot of what I wore came from sources like the church's free box. At the end of Sunday night service, there'd be bags of odds and ends that people had left behind for the poor, which my dad proudly gleaned, with thanks to God for providing. Then I'd end up wearing another kid's hand-me-downs to Sunday school, much to my chagrin.

A buxom, well-dressed girl named Christina was in our church choir. She was about fourteen or so when I met her and she wore cool cat glasses with her hair styled in a perfect page boy. She always sat with the other popular girls and the cutest boys in the back row at choir practice, giggling a lot, whispering and chewing gum, which stirred up a whole mixture of feelings in me, from fear, to envy, to disdain, wishing only that they would let me be part of their little group.

At the tender age of eleven I was awkward anyhow, and always extra self-conscious around Christina, feeling positive that she and her friends were snickering and talking about me behind my back. I was sure that the bizarre combinations of polyester flowers and plaids I wore, with badly-fitting shoes and my rat's nest of tangled hair, made me really quite ridiculous. And I knew I smelled funny, too. Everyone in my house smelled funny, like cat pee.

One day after Sunday service my dad told me we were going to drop by Christina's house on the way home. "But why?" I asked apprehensively.

"Oh, Christina's mother says she has a bag of clothes Christina grew out of that you can have! Isn't that nice of them?"

"Oh that's great," I said, hoping they wouldn't be home.

"Why don't you run up there and get the stuff and come back to the car. I'll just wait here."

I ran up the steps, rang the bell and Christina answered the door, wearing jeans and a groovy tight t-shirt, chewing gum as usual, with the phone in one hand. "Mom!" She yelled, while I stood there. "Someone's at the door!" Then she just walked away, like she'd never seen me before.

"Oh, hello dear. Here's some things Christina's grown out of that might fit you one day…I mean, that you could maybe wear…Well here they are. See you next Sunday!"

I grabbed the bag from the floor beside Christina's mom's dainty, pedicured foot and dashed back to my dad, smiling in the car.

"Well you've got yourself a great big bag of clothes there, eh? That Christina sure is a nice, pretty girl to give you her clothes like that. Aren't you lucky?"

At home I scurried up to my room with the bag, to survey my new wardrobe. Recognizing some of the outfits I'd seen Christina wear at church, I shuddered, and thought of how she might react, seeing me wearing her clothes.

A long blue cotton dress didn't seem too bad, though, and I slipped it over my head, surveying the fit from all angles in the mirror. Taking a tuck here and there with some safety pins, I figured it was probably the best thing I owned and I thought I looked quite good.

I didn't fill it out like Christina did, but I liked the color, it wasn't wrinkled, and it smelled nice too. It was sleeveless and my skinny arms were a little lost in all that fabric. The arm holes were pretty big, but there was a tie at the back and I bunched up the excess there, so you could hardly tell the dress wasn't made for me.

The darts on front for the bustline were an unnecessary detail, which just got pulled around the sides, so I thought it all looked like just part of the design. The only shoes I had were kind of old and worn, but you could hardly see them, because the dress was long. I wouldn't even have to wear socks!

"Are you going to come down and model one of your outfits for us?" my dad bellowed from the living room.

"Yeah, okay. Here I come!"

My brother Michael snickered when I appeared in the dress and my dad, ignoring him, said, "Well, that looks real pretty on you! Are you going to wear it to Easter Service next Sunday?"

"I might. Yeah, I think I will. And I'll even do something fancy with my hair."

"Good girl. There you go," my dad said, looking proud.

Easter Sunday morning I brushed my hair into a high pony tail and used a clip one of my aunties had given me to pin my bangs to one side. The dress looked really stylish and I thought maybe even

Christina would think so. Maybe she'd even be envious that I looked so good in something she'd "grown out of." Maybe even some of her friends would want to talk to me. I thought that they'd invite me to giggle and chew gum in the back row with them and I'd accept their invitation, maybe.

When we lined up for choir, I stood in my usual place at the front, watching as the others filed by to take their places behind. Christina's face flashed surprise as she walked past, noticing me wearing her beautiful dress. I hoped she wasn't too jealous, so I smiled brightly to let her know we were friends, but she only stared coldly and walked to the back row with the other girls.

A knot grew in the pit of my stomach and I suddenly knew I looked ridiculous, just like always.

They were already starting to giggle. Their giggling got louder and continued through every song. I couldn't tell if it was them or if the giggling was in my head, but I felt like throwing up and my face burned with held-in tears. Easter service felt like an eternity.

As we walked off the stage when the service ended, I heard Christina whisper to a girl as they passed me, "Look at that. Pitiful isn't she?" They snorted all the way down the aisle, glancing back at me, holding their hands over their mouths to contain their laughter.

I died a little inside, then ran home, threw the dress in the garbage and climbed under the covers with my cats.

"Did anyone tell you how pretty you looked at church today?" my dad asked hopefully.

"Yeah, they loved it," I lied.

Somehow I just couldn't tell him that they'd laughed at my dress and called me pitiful. I didn't want to see him hurt for me.

BECOMING REAL

I can relate to the story of the Velveteen Rabbit. Rabbit doesn't think he's much of anything compared to the other fancy toys. He mostly gets ignored by the little boy he belongs to and when the Skin Horse tells Rabbit about being real, the Rabbit both longs for and is afraid of how becoming real might hurt.

"Generally, by the time you are Real, most of your hair has been loved off. Your eyes drop out and you get loose in the joints and very shabby," says the Skin Horse. The Rabbit, much as he likes the idea of becoming Real, feels it's risky and wishes he could become Real without uncomfortable things happening to him.

"It doesn't happen all at once," said the Skin Horse. "You become. It takes a long time. That's why it doesn't happen often to people who break easily, or have sharp edges, or who have to be carefully kept. But these things don't matter at all, because once you are Real you can't be ugly, except to people who don't understand."

I remember feeling like the Velveteen Rabbit when I was a little girl. I was shabby and smelly compared to the other girls with their crisp dresses, white socks and shiny hair. They all seemed so much better than me. I carried the thought with me for many, many years, that I just wasn't lovable. But under my sadness was something real trying to come out.

Such is life and love and becoming real. It's not comfortable. It's risky to love and be loved. Over time, I've let love in. Bit by bit, I've softened. Bit by bit, my fur has been loved off.

Sure becoming real hurts sometimes, but we're worth it.

Uncle Sunny

I always called him Uncle Sunny, which is what my dad called his younger brother Richard, probably because he was a little guy and my dad had to protect him from getting beaten up when they were kids. Most likely, the spelling was "Sonny," but not to me.

Other people in the family called him Mickey. His beautiful wife Gloria's nickname was Glo. To my child's mind, Sunny and Glo glowed and they were two people who belonged together, just like the sun and moon.

They were like movie stars to me, with their good looks and interesting life, selling flashy mobile homes and spending whatever time they could on the old classic yacht they lovingly restored.

We got to go out on the boat sometimes, too. I have great memories of anchoring off the BC coast and Gloria putting me in a life jacket, with a rope tied to it so I could bob around in the water and not get lost. I think that's where I first got my love of boats and the ocean and those memories will always be close to my heart.

Uncle Sunny could fix or build anything. I remember the story of how he and Aunt Glo got started as two young kids in love who had nothing. They lived in an old trailer and my cousins Penny and Roger, when they were babies, slept in a dresser drawer.

"We fixed that old trailer real good and we sold it for more than we paid for it. I painted it all up, Gloria made new curtains and she looked like a brand new rig!" he'd say proudly. "Then we just kept doing that, over and over, till we had a little bit of money, and the rest is history."

I loved that story, as much for the way it spoke of humble beginnings, as for its showing how caring for something in need of TLC can give it new life. My deep belief in redemption is right at my core and as a child, seeing tangible examples of little things Uncle Sunny repaired helped form some of that foundation in me.

Our family – my dad, brother and I – saw Sunny and Glo and Grandma quite often, because they all lived on the trailer lot. We went there most Sundays for dinner and while the adults were visiting, my brother Michael and I played around all the shiny new mobile homes and I'd have a blast roller skating around the big expanse of black asphalt.

When I was about seven, visiting Sunny and Glo one Sunday afternoon, Sunny, still in his coveralls and finishing work for the day, noticed my crappy worn-down shoes. We'd come straight from church, so I was still wearing my only pair of shoes, a black patent leather "Mary Jane" style, at least a size too big for me. I didn't notice that I had beaten down the backs of them with my heels, probably to make them feel more comfortable and so they'd stay on my feet.

"Hey!" Uncle Sunny called to me, wiping his hands on a rag. "What's wrong with your shoes? Those don't look too comfortable. Come here, let me take a look at them," he said, bending my leg at the knee, then lifting my foot, like I was a horse to be shod. I felt a little ashamed of my run down shoes, while at the same time, my Uncle's loving attention made my heart feel all giddy.

"Oh, these shoes need some work done on them. Why don't you come in the shop with me and I'll fix them for you," he said, patting my head. Inside the big shop it smelled of paint and solvent and rubber. "You can sit up here," Sunny said, pulling up a tall stool for me.

I watched him carefully turn the shoes over in his hands, measure them, then he measured my feet, too. The heels of the shoes were worn down on the bottom, so he cut pieces of heavy rubber, glued one under each shoe and used a big sanding wheel to smooth it all out, just like they were made that way.

Next, Uncle Sunny got pieces of thick leather, cut them and glued two thicknesses together, putting that inside the heels at the back of each shoe and gluing them in. "Those will have to dry for a bit, so let's go have supper and check on them afterwards, eh? I'll bring them back to the house."

When supper was done, Uncle Sunny handed the shoes back to me. He'd buffed them to a shine with black polish and they didn't even look like my shoes at all.

"Wow! They fit! They look like new!" I squealed. "How did you do that? Thank you, Uncle Sunny!"

"Anything can be fixed if you do it right. Waste not, want not, eh?" he said, "Remember that."

I will always remember that. Nothing and no one is beyond redemption.

STAGES, TIMING
· · · · · AND THE RIGHT CARE · · · · ·

For the past few days I've been snuffling and coughing with a cold. It's right out of the pages of one of my Chinese medicine textbooks: "wind cold external pathogenic influence." I even saw it coming, because of how I'd been going along, not taking proper care of myself: I got cold, I got wet, I got tired, I got stressed; and now, here was a nasty cold to make me slow down and reconsider how I can be sensitive to my body. I get to learn once more, humbly, from my own example, how everything in life has its stages and timing.

A cold has stages and East-Asian medicine treats each stage differently, according to how the body is manifesting the illness at the time. For example, my cold started with chills and a headache. The right care at this stage — to warm and "sweat out" the pathogen, using acupuncture, herbs and some spicy foods like ginger and scallions — will often nip a cold in the bud and it will be gone. Usually I can do this successfully, if I catch it at the right stage.

But when the cold goes deeper and fever sets in, fluids thicken and become difficult to move, so a cough and stuffy nose result. The throat gets sore and everything starts to dry up. Treatment is different now, aimed at cooling, moistening and loosening stuck mucus. I taught my husband to do gua sha on my back, a technique of scraping the skin with a piece of jade to release heat and fever. It helped a lot.

Later on, the stage I'm at now, there may be dampness and cold again, because the body gets weakened by fighting the pathogen. Yang has been used up by all the coughing and fever. The treatment is gentle warming, nourishing with ginger soup to dry excess fluids, along with rest and using moxa, a stick of burning herb passed closely over the skin, to chase dampness from the channels, which is what I'll be doing today. By tomorrow I should be mostly back to my old self. Knock on wood.

A cold will run its course in a week or less, though like many things, emotions included, if one stage is not properly addressed, it can go on and on. I've had plenty of two-month colds from trying to "ignore" or "push through" when my body was saying a clear "No." I've also experienced a lot of times when emotions like grief have cycled for a very long time in my soul because I didn't honor the stage I was in with the right care.

We're all different. We experience life differently and so there is no "one size fits all" solution, even with something as common as a cold.

. . . .

Socks

All the other little girls at school had clean white socks and I didn't. I had holey, mismatched "pairs" of grayish ones with no elastic left in them, so they piled up in my gumboots, which I wore to hide my sub-par socks. We were poor and my dad was sad a lot, so I guess that's why he didn't notice certain things about how we were dressed or what we lacked.

At one point, I remember not having any underwear and I went looking in my brother's drawers, finding a pair of his, with the opening in the front to pee from. I figured no one would notice if I wore them. Kids can be mean though, and one day while changing after gym class in grade three, one of the girls saw my strange undergarments and pointed me out to everyone screaming, "Oooo, look at her boy's undies! Oooo!" I changed in the bathroom stall from then on.

It must have been a Christmas or birthday present, but I got a pair of long, pure-white knee socks and a pair of crisp white panties. I was thrilled and felt that finally I'd be able to join the same league as the other girls. I proudly wore my new socks to school, showing them off by wearing my black patent-leather "Sunday-school" shoes, so everyone would see that I too had gleaming, white socks.

In order to keep them white, I had to wash my precious socks every night in the bathroom sink, where I stood on a stool, scrubbing the socks on a washboard, with a big bar of lemon soap. In warmer weather, they'd be mostly dry by morning if I hung them outside on the clothesline and if the weather was cold and wet, I'd lay them on the heat register, hoping the furnace would kick in enough to get them dry. I wondered if that's what all the other little girls were doing each night to keep their socks so white and clean. It didn't even cross my mind that maybe they had more than one pair of fresh white socks.

Years later, I was talking to a man at Seattle's Harborview Hospital who'd just had surgery to amputate all of his toes. He was a Vietnam veteran who was homeless and living on the street at a time when the weather was cold and wet. One evening he'd been walking a long way in the snow and rain, finally stopping to sleep in his makeshift tent of plastic and cardboard. The temperature dropped to freezing that night and when he woke up, his toes in those wet socks were frozen solid.

Having a pair or two of clean dry socks can be a crucial "luxury" for someone who doesn't have much else to comfort them. A clean pair of socks can keep a person with a low immune system from getting sick and keep their toes from freezing off when winter sets in. This cold weather season, your gift of socks to someone who needs them can boost morale and help them get through another day. When you live on the street, having warm dry feet is essential to wellbeing and in the harsh world of living outside, socks are more than just something to put on your feet.

—————— INVISIBLE ——————

The way I grew up, there were a lot of times I felt like there was nobody there for me. As a little kid I was often left alone because my dad had to work, my mom was gone and there was no one to care for me when I was sick. Abuse and other things I didn't understand happened at our house in my presence, as if I wasn't there, as if it didn't matter whether I saw or heard what was going on. I felt invisible.

Feeling invisible turned into my belief that no one cared and I wasn't worth caring about. For many years I carried those beliefs with me and I built other beliefs, becoming supersensitive to criticism and alert for the slightest look that I could interpret as, "You don't think I matter." Then when I'd figure I was picking up on someone's opinion of me, I'd get hostile, but usually not express it. Instead I'd just implode, hate myself and hate anyone who triggered my sad, limiting beliefs.

Recently I was at a meeting with a group who were interested in some of the trauma integration trainings I do. I was explaining about what I teach and my philosophy about trauma and we were having a good discussion. As if he hadn't heard the conversation we'd been having, someone started speaking about another person who does trauma training, which I was interested to hear about. Then he said, "I hate bad trainers, so I think we should use this other person for our training sessions."

As he kept talking, I was aware of a familiar, hollow sort of feeling in my gut. Was he talking about me? Was I invisible for him to speak like this, as if I wasn't there? I kept trying to catch his eye as he spoke, to check out if I was hearing him correctly. What he was saying sounded like I was being dismissed and even insulted, but knowing my own history, I didn't want to project my old business. Still, he avoided my eyes, even though we were right across from each other.

This felt important and I didn't want to react to what I was feeling, in case I was reading too much into his words, but I was curious about the feeling I'd had in my gut, that familiar feeling telling me to pay attention. I knew it was healing for me to pause and register how I felt. I remembered. My body remembered. My nervous system remembered the original trauma and the root of my old beliefs, yet there was also some part of me that also felt okay.

I had noticed what he'd said, then I had second guessed myself, so I didn't speak up to question my assumption about what I thought I'd heard. I decided instead to sit with it and examine the feeling in my gut, which reminded me of old trauma and beliefs. At the same time, I somehow didn't feel traumatized. It was like watching a movie rather than being in the movie, or like waking up from a dream. I saw something clearer than I've ever seen it, just from the catalyst of someone's words.

It may seem like a lot of noise for just one little observation, but the light shone on a dark corner of me today and I celebrate the continued integration of my wholeness. This kind of epiphany is a small personal miracle, and though I may still have the baggage, at least I know I'm carrying it and can put it down if I choose. I'm not invisible. I am here.

The Park

When I was an awkward eleven-year-old, I'd go to the park after church on Sundays, just a block from our house. There were expansive playing fields and the playground had two sets of swings, monkey bars, teeter totters, a sandbox and concrete pool that was filled during summer months. And there was a little brick house near the pool for the park custodian. That's where George lived.

One day I was sitting on the swings alone, kicking the dust, when George came out to pick up some trash and saw me, saying loudly in his broad Scottish brogue, "Hi there beautiful girl! Why so sad today?" I looked around, figuring he must be speaking to a beautiful girl, because no one had ever called little scruffy me, "beautiful." But he walked up and looked right at me. "Yes, you!" he laughed. "Want to come inside where it's warm and have some tea?"

I looked at him, trying to figure out if he was being fatherly or something else...

All my senses started prickling, telling me to run. I remember the pulling in my gut, telling me to get away as fast as I could, but instead I shrugged and said, "Sure." I was curious, rebellious and, most of all, I was used to pushing away my own protective instincts. Danger drew me in like a magnet.

Inside, George took my coat, hung it up and said, "Oh, how about some orange juice instead? I think I'm out of tea just now."

"Okay, that's fine," I said, fighting panic that I'd gotten myself into a bad situation. He handed me a glass of orange juice, poured himself half a glass, then took a vodka bottle from the cupboard, filling his glass the rest of the way with booze.

I tried to look nonchalant and sipped my juice, sizing up the doorway and calculating how fast I could run, though my feet seemed like they were glued to the floor and a familiar feeling of quickly hardening concrete filled my throat and chest.

"Do you want to play cards?" he asked me.

"Okay," I said, a bit relieved. "I only know how to play one game where you just keep putting cards down and the person with the highest card takes the pile and you just keep going till all the cards are gone."

"Oh, sure, that sounds good," George said. "If you win, I'll give you five dollars per game. If I win, you have to give me a kiss."

"You won't ever get to kiss me," I challenged. "I'll kick your ass at cards every time."

He smiled broadly. "I like your fighting spirit little one! You can cut the deck."

I won, took my five bucks, said "no" to "a little vodka" in my orange juice and ran all the way home. "See you again soon I hope!" George called after me. I shuddered in my bed that night, vowing to never go to the park again.

Next Sunday, though, I was sitting on the swings, waiting for George to invite me in to play cards. Within a few minutes, there he was. "Come on in then, what are you waiting for? Here, have some vodka. It has no smell, no one will ever know."

We sat and talked for a long time. He talked about being in the war and having a wife and kids, whose photo was on the table. "But they all left me. I'm just an old bastard," he trailed off. He asked about me, like what I did at school, my friends, my cats. "Aye, I like cats too. I used to have an orange tabby, but he died. I miss him, too..." he said with a drunken tear in his eye. In spite of it all, I found myself feeling sorry for him and as we sat there chatting, I started to like the old bastard.

Soon I was hanging out with George, getting drunk every Sunday afternoon at his place while, just up the street, my dad snoozed in his lazy boy and my brother Michael sat watching TV, oblivious to my escapades at the park. My reckless antics were surely rebellion and also a plea for someone to notice how much I hurt, how much I hated myself, but no one did seem to notice.

I wasn't afraid of much in those days anyhow. My dad was an assistant pastor at our church and he often took me with him to one of his church ministries in Vancouver's Downtown Lower-Eastside. Hanging out in dark alleys so my dad could preach and play harmonica for anyone who'd listen, these "street meetings" were a regular outing for my dad and me from the time I could walk and there was no shortage of characters in those dark alleys to scare most little girls.

My dad told me not to be scared, though, and I wasn't. "They're all God's children, just like you and me," he'd say. I guess that's why to me, George was no more scary than a lot of characters and dirty old men I'd met.

I kept beating him at cards, most times anyhow. And when I lost, I kept my side of the deal and let the old bugger kiss me, without even knowing why I was consenting to it. "Yuck!" I'd sneer. "You're gross!"

George would laugh and I'd take off, staggering home to flop on the couch with the cats to sleep it off. We had a strange sort of "friendship" if you could call it that, though I can't believe neighbors wouldn't have noticed me lurching along, stopping to throw up or lay on the boulevard after an afternoon of guzzling vodka.

Eventually George was fired from his position when he was reported for buying booze for minors, like he did for my friend Kathy and me when we were going to a party. I feel bad that he got fired and hoped it wasn't my fault. Truth be told, I even missed him when he was gone. The park was never the same after that and I don't think I was either.

———— REGRET AND REMORSE ————

Regret and remorse seem different in quality, though both look back over a shoulder at something, either done or not done, which we wish had been otherwise. Remorse has a type of sorrow to it. If we feel remorse for something, we experience a type of reckoning, a clarity about how our actions, words, deeds have affected another. We let down the wall of protection we use for keeping us "right" and we admit our frailty with open hands.

In court proceedings, a judge may base the sentence for a crime on whether the accused shows remorse for what has been committed. Remorse, in retrospect, matters to us.

Regret has another quality. It comes more from a mind that knows there's no going back, rather than from the heart full of sorrow and the desire to make things better. Regret may come when we wish things in the past had been different, yet we know we cannot change it now.

I have learned to know remorse in a personal way, discovering it as an evolution of my selfish words and actions, into awareness that I've hurt someone. There was a time when remorse would flicker through me and I'd ignore it so I didn't have to feel my own pain, let alone another's. Now knowing I hurt someone hurts me too. True, heartfelt remorse can be a cleansing.

Regret is really just a waste of time and even though I try to live life without it, it still comes up when I second guess myself.

Loved

He yelled at us when he was mad. He had a bad temper and my brother was the one who got the brunt of it, but there was one time that my dad tried to spank me.

I was about four years old and I think I lied about something, which was grounds for punishment. I have a vague memory of his hand hitting my backside several times, then he stopped and stood me in front of him. We stared at one another, me dry-eyed and defiant, he with tears in his eyes.

It was the first and last time I got a spanking. He could see it wasn't going to work with me...

We were at Queen Elizabeth Park one Sunday afternoon, walking around with all the other people, admiring the quarry gardens, all abloom in spring flowers. My dad loved flowers and trees, so we came here a lot.

As we stood on the archway over the stream, I was clutching a small pocket knife I'd found in a puddle on my way home from school. The pocket knife had been rusty and bent, but it caught my eye and shone at me, asking to be saved, so I brought it home.

My dad said, "Oh that looks like a good little knife. Let's boil it to clean it and get some steel wool to shine it up. Then we can put some oil on the hinge and it'll be good as new." I guess that's part of the reason I loved that little knife, the way the tiny blade folded in so snug and how it shone, grateful that I rescued it and had seen its hidden beauty.

The other part of why a little girl would love a pocket knife, why I loved the knife, was because of how my dad had so tenderly and lovingly helped me clean it, restore it and make it like new. That was the special part really. Yes, that's why I loved the knife.

Standing there on the little wooden bridge with my dad, leaning over the side so I could view the expansive gardens, I couldn't help taking the knife out of my pocket and turning it in the sunlight as it glinted and winked at me. Then it slipped from my hands, dropping over the railing, tinkling its way across the rocks, far down the straight drop to the stream below, where it landed on a mossy ledge.

My dad must have been watching me when I dropped the knife. He must have seen the shock and sadness in my face, because then, without a word, my dad, all two-hundred-and-fifty pounds of him, in his Sunday best, took off his shoes and socks, rolled up his pant legs and began to hike down the steep bank.

There were a bunch of signs that said, "No climbing on rocks; Stay off the rocks" but my dad paid no attention to those signs.

People were looking at him. I think someone took a photo of the big, fat man, climbing on the dangerous rocks with no shoes on. No one knew what he was doing except me and I couldn't have been more proud of my dad. He looked graceful, the way he carefully stepped, weaving back and forth over the stream, purposefully moving among the rocks.

Graceful, like a dancer, he moved down then up the cliff, wiping his brow once or twice, smiling up at me – just for me – so I'd see he really didn't mind doing me this favor, letting me know it was really his pleasure to show his love in this way.

My shiny pocket knife was tucked into his suit pocket and when he was back at the top, he picked up his shoes, sat on a bench, slowly dried his feet and put his shoes back on.

"Here," he said, giving it a wipe dry with his handkerchief. "Hold on to it better next time."

"Thank you Daddy." And that was all either of us said.

Sexual abuse, violence and neglect were all part of our daily lives growing up in that house, but love was also there. I have memories of all of it, the good, the bad, the ugly and the love I felt from my dad.

People are complicated, as my husband reminds me so often. Relationships are complicated and the ones with our parents are probably the most complicated, so I'm grateful to have some good things to remember.

And no matter what else happened, I know I was loved.

The Front Porch

I was fortunate to live my first thirteen years in a house. Some kids don't even have a home, much less a house to live in. Being able to come back from school and walk in the door was definitely a blessing, giving me a sense of stability, in the midst of a chaotic environment.

Our green house was a veteran's home, one of six or so styles in the several-mile radius of our neighborhood. When my dad got out of the air force, he and other service men were able to purchase homes for their families for five thousand dollars, to help them get a start in civilian life. Thank goodness for that.

If I was an artist, I could easily draw it right now. I remember every detail, every inch of the house inside and out. I remember the yard, the front walkway with a crack in it, the walkway I'd run down, jumping into my dad's arms when he came home.

For years it was like that: my dad, with his big smile, getting out of the car and standing there with open arms, ready to sweep me up. I loved him so fiercely then...My brother, too, ran to his arms. He'd carry us both into the house and make our dinner. Over time things changed and one day it wasn't like that anymore. None of us were content or happy when the abuse started.

The front of the house had a narrow garden strip facing south, in full sun, and a hose spigot with the handle missing. My sister told me years later that Mom loved to garden and she'd fill that area with tomatoes, onions and flowers like sweet peas, because they smelled so good. I never saw those things, just weeds, which we were told to pull out once in a while, until one day my dad stopped telling us to do even that.

There were just too many weeds.

My dad always painted our front porch in bright colors. It was blue for the longest time, an almost neon blue that I could see all the way from my elementary school across the field. I'd walk along slitting my eyes nearly closed, until the steps were a blue beacon I followed home.

One Saturday morning he opened a gallon of red enamel paint. "You kids can help me. We're going to paint the porch red, like a regal carpet for the Queen. Maybe she'll even pay us a visit one day!" he said wistfully. A true monarchist, my dad loved the Queen.

The front porch was where we'd yell and bang pots and pans to bring in the New Year, much to the chagrin of some of our neighbors. And on Halloween, my dad brought home bricks of firecrackers and other fireworks, which we'd gleefully throw off the porch into the night sky. I wondered if the Queen would have enjoyed that...

All three of us had brushes, dipping them in the big can of red enamel and slopping over the blue. It was fun and I liked how we were all doing something normal and constructive together.

Not sure why it's so clear for me still, but I remember the smell of coal in the air. Usually you only smelled it in winter, when people were burning it to keep warm. Yet here it was today in the summer, a strange, acrid smell that made the back of my throat feel numb.

I went inside to get a drink and when I came out, there was just a small unpainted spot for me to step, in order to get past my dad, so I could pick up my brush again. I lifted my foot, sure that I would nimbly hop over the painted area.

"No!" was all I heard. Then I was tumbling, sliding along the red enamel, feeling myself becoming covered in the sticky red goo, until I thudded onto the sidewalk. I hit my head and when my eyes opened, all I could see was the paint can on its side and red paint pouring into the dirt, beside where I lay.

I don't know who yelled. I thought I knew, but now as I recollect, I'm not sure if it was my dad, my brother, my imagination, or some sense of doubt in me that heard the "No."

Without a word, my dad picked me up in his arms and carried me around to the back porch and into the kitchen. I was crying and scared from the fall. I was afraid of the mess I'd made. My hair, arms, legs, my favorite cut offs and t-shirt, were all ruined, plus the paint was wasted and the porch looked even worse than I did, with a skid-marked imprint of my body right through the middle of it.

"We have more paint," he said quietly. "This is turpentine to clean your arms and legs. Here's some on a cloth. Wipe your hair. It's okay. You didn't do anything wrong. I'm not mad at you."

Where did he learn such gentleness?

I guess that's why this day is still vivid for me, so many years later. My dad gave me gentleness and care I doubt he'd received as a child. That's the part I keep thinking of. No one showed him how to be a good parent. A lot of the time he was anything but a good parent, but then there were moments like this.

We always remember how someone made us feel.

And somehow on this day, my dad knew exactly how to show me that I mattered, more than the paint did.

——— PAIN ———

We are born with a natural human instinct to avoid pain and our nervous systems pull us away from fire when we feel too much heat. With difficult emotions, we try to avoid feeling pain by shutting down a part of ourselves. We deny what we feel because we are terrified the pain may never stop. Even if we try to keep the lid on pain for years, decades or even an entire lifetime, pain seeps out as anger, violence, depression, shame, addiction and, under it all, fear.

We hurt one another and most of all we hurt ourselves. Great gentleness is needed to stop the cycle and we may not be used to gentleness and patience, especially for ourselves, especially when it's not the way we've done things and not the way much of the world operates.

But if we choose to do something different, by noticing our feelings, breathing and seeing how our long held beliefs may not fit anymore, we may begin to trust ourselves. Somewhere deep, a sense of possibility stirs. We discover that healing is a natural consequence of our awareness.

Having and Being

It seemed like anytime I let down my guard and started feeling okay, something bad would happen, like my oldest brother, fresh out of prison, busting our door down and threatening everyone. In the rage of his yelling and cursing was always the accusation: "You all have everything and I have nothing!"

An insidious idea formed in my consciousness: having something is wrong, bad or even dangerous.

Not only should I not have anything good, or something that no one else around me had, but I shouldn't be anything that could cause jealousy in others. Even if I was just feeling okay when others weren't...that could also put me at risk.

Having something good or being something good made me a target.

Deconstructing this belief, I remember how my brother Michael would become angry if I won at checkers, soccer in the backyard, Monopoly...Or if I got a present or approval that he didn't get, that was enough for him to see red. I got beat up daily, just for being me.

My dad told me: "Don't win so many races at the church picnic. Let the other kids get some ribbons, too."

"Don't color that picture so nicely. The other kids will feel bad."

"Who do you think you are?"

Seems it wasn't just me carrying that belief...

It wasn't safe to have or be perceived as more than or better than. I understood that being small was the road of least resistance. Having less or nothing, though it hurt, still felt safer.

I kept carrying the idea through my teen years, feeling that I was protecting myself by blending in and twisting myself to conform. I was loyal to my fear and I lost myself along the way.

Years ago while talking with a friend I said, "Oh well, you can't have anything." We both laughed, knowing what I'd meant to say was

"Oh well, you can't have everything." But then again, there was some truth to the first way I'd said it. Deep down I still believed I couldn't, or shouldn't, have anything.

I've noticed with beliefs, that when you start to see through them, they become flimsy and are not nearly as intact as they once were.

Years later, I can imagine how my brother felt. No one visited David in jail. He spent years there, beginning in his teens, and he kept returning. I don't even know why he was in jail but I know that when he came back to the only home he'd ever known, he wasn't welcome, so he raged, accused and threatened, trying to be heard.

And Michael was angry at the abuse he suffered, so he lashed out at me because I was closest.

Their rage was not about me.

I wish I knew then what I know now.

Cat Mary

Once church was done, we'd often spend Sunday afternoons driving around Richmond, where my dad worked part time driving cab. He'd gotten to know a lot of the very poor people who lived on the outskirts, befriending them and inevitably talking to them about Jesus. And since we were on the way to Grandma's house for dinner, there was no way out of going along on these "mission visits," which was what we did most Sundays. My dad considered one of his duties as an assistant pastor at our church was to care for the very poor and even though we were also poor, we gave them whatever we could.

My most vivid memory is of a woman called "Cat Mary," who lived in a bramble-covered shack on the Fraser River mud flats. The falling-down tin hovel was overrun by at least a hundred runny-eyed cats, all meowing and jumping around between the stacks of smelly newspapers and other garbage.

I never saw any furniture or appliances, so I never knew where she slept or if she had a bathroom or kitchen. It seemed like Cat Mary just slept on the newspapers with the cats and maybe she ate their food, too.

Whenever we came to see her, Cat Mary would run to my dad with open arms, toothlessly grinning and giggling like a school girl. Her clothes were filthy, her hair was matted and she smelled like she bathed in cat pee, yet Cat Mary's eyes sparkled, never seeming self-conscious in the slightest.

On the way there, we'd usually stop at McDonalds to buy Mary a Big Mac, as well as some groceries and cat food, for which she would thank my dad a thousand times. Embarrassed to be thanked so much, he'd pull out his harmonica and sing "The Green, Green Grass of Home" to her, crooning like Tom Jones himself.

"Down the road I look and there runs Mary, hair of gold and lips like cherries…"

I'm pretty sure he was thinking of my mom when he sang, but Mary would clasp her hands together, with stars in her eyes. I really loved my dad at moments like that.

Mary always fussed over me, cooing and clucking, while petting my hair in the same way she stroked the cats crawling over her torn apron. I didn't mind. In fact I liked the attention, though my brother, Michael, kept his distance, not daring to come in. Instead, he usually wandered around picking berries by the fence out back, probably counting the minutes until we could leave.

She seemed so fragile and thin, so childlike in her simple devotion to all those cats, that even as a young child I felt oddly maternal and protective towards Mary. Once in a while, she'd offer a kitten as "payment" for the food we brought and though it was the last thing we needed, we'd end up driving away with another kitty, to add to our already ridiculous number of cats.

At night I sometimes dreamed of Mary. I think it was partly

because my mom's name was Mary, too, and in my dreams images twisted into an eerie hybrid of the two women, calling me.

My heart hurt whenever we had to leave Mary there. I'd sit in the back seat with a new kitten on my lap, watching out the back window as we drove away, with Mary waving till we were out of sight.

When I closed my eyes, her image was still there – the outline of her raised hand, bony shoulders, bare feet and ragged dress.

Loss swept over me again.

I could never understand why we weren't taking Mary with us.

BELIEF

Healing trauma is arguably most effective if we start with examining specific events when we most likely formed the beliefs controlling our life. Beliefs comes from thoughts collected together and expressed repetitively, whether the expression is to others or just kept as our own private hell.

Thoughts and feelings are closely related, but not the same. Thoughts are a response to something happening in our life, which stimulates an emotional response. Sometimes it's the other way around and emotions come first, stimulating thoughts.

We can create entire structures of how we believe life is, who we are, what others think of us, why others respond to us the way that they do, what the world is and what our role is in it.

We don't just create beliefs, we project them onto the world. Pretty soon everyone and everything conforms to our beliefs and this becomes our reality. We cling to what we have created. We are righteous. In our minds, we absolutely believe our own story. We become rigid, like the freeze response of some long ago trauma. Helpless, powerless, threatened.

I have done many things over the years to try to unlock my stuck beliefs: group therapy, individual therapy, genograms, rebirthing, sweat lodge, meditation, yoga, plant medicine, EFT, EMDR and so many more things I can't even remember. Every single intervention I've used has brought me to the same place – the stark realization that my beliefs control my life, if I let them.

It's humbling.

Where did this belief start? Specifically, where and when did I get the ideas that became my beliefs, and why?

What happened?

Is there a belief you cling to which hobbles you in life?

Timmy

One of my first friends, when we were both about five, was a boy named Timmy. He lived down the street, across from the park, in one of the bland veterans homes like ours. Timmy's dad was a fireman and his sister Trudy was a year older than me, rounded and pretty, with silky blond hair, unlike my fuzzy mop. I wanted to be her friend too, but she barely tolerated me, with my scruffy clothes and wild enthusiasm for all the things her little brother liked, such as dirt, Matchbox cars and toy guns. I didn't mind though, because Timmy loved me and I loved him.

Timmy and I spent a lot of time together. I can close my eyes right now and see his wide smile and big brown crew-cut head. I'd rub my hand across the soft bristly hairs and say, "Furry, furry Timmy," which always made him laugh. He let me ride on his back around their yard, patting his head until his mom would call us in to eat.

Often lunch was Campbell's tomato soup, something we never had at my house. I was fascinated by how Timmy's mom used a clean dishcloth to wipe the crumbs from the plastic tablecloth, sweeping them into her other hand. At my house, no one wiped the table like that and things just ended up on the floor.

Timmy, me, Trudy and Dad and Michael, all dressed in our Crusader Uniforms

Timmy's mom hugged me often, like I was one of her kids, and she called me "Sweetie," which made me feel all feminine and pretty for some reason. I think it was how she said it, with a faraway look in her eyes, almost sad...I don't know. I was just a kid, but I do remember her face looking worn and weary, reminding me of Alice Kramden on the Honeymooners, when Ralph would yell at her...

That's what I thought way back then. I figured she was sad and that her fireman husband must yell at her.

Weird, how kids think.

I loved being at their house as much as I could and Timmy would come over to my house lots, too, tagging along on Sunday outings after church. He even joined "Crusaders" with me, the evangelical church's answer to Boy Scouts and Girl Guides, just so we could spend more time together.

Timmy and I were in love. I think in a past lifetime he was my husband.

We were soulmates.

In elementary school we grew apart, and Timmy joined military cadets, later went into the army and then we lost touch.

Years later I was on a crowded bus in Vancouver and a young man in uniform was standing next to me, holding onto the railing and preparing to get off, when our eyes met.

"Timmy?" I said, instinctively reaching to touch his crew-cut head, my fingers slipping through the soft bristles.

"Hi," he said, grinning that same smile, reaching up to touch my hand.

"I miss you."

"Me too."

"I gotta get off here."

"Okay. Bye"

"Yeah. Bye"

It was the last time I ever saw him.

—— FAITH AND SURRENDER ——

What is faith and what is surrender? Martial arts legend Bruce Lee once said: "Empty your cup so that it may be filled; become devoid to gain totality." What does emptying one's cup mean? What is it to be empty and how can we "do" such a thing? How can we have the faith to surrender? What comes next?

We cannot "do" emptiness but we can cultivate the ability to surrender what we hold in our minds and, therefore, our bodies. As Max Strom wisely says in his beautiful book, A Life Worth Breathing: "Nothing happens in the mind that doesn't happen in the body. They are one."

For most of us, the last time we really felt free, safe and surrendered was when we were still in the womb. So now what? Isn't it "natural" to defend and hold on? Or are we just in the habit of resisting rather than letting go? What are we so afraid of losing?

We can make a conscious dedication to awareness with something like meditation, prayer, art, athletics, music, dance. There are so many paths to "lose" our minds as we devote attention and heart to almost anything. The key is finding enough curiosity for a tiny bit of faith (like a grain of mustard seed) to allow our surrender. It takes faith in the unknown. It's not logical. Surrender allows faith. Faith allows surrender.

Sexual Abuse and Addiction

In his bestselling book on addiction, *In The Realm of Hungry Ghosts*, Dr. Gabor Maté tells of his work serving addicts living on Vancouver's mean streets: "I don't have a single female patient in the Downtown Eastside of Vancouver who wasn't sexually abused, for example, as were many of the men, or abused, neglected and abandoned serially, over and over again. That's what sets up the brain biology of addiction. In other words, the addiction is related both psychologically, in terms of emotional pain relief, and neurobiological development to early adversity."

On some level, we know this stark truth already, even if our awareness of it is buried deep in our unconscious. We see the hollow faces of people on the streets. We can imagine that something terrible must have happened to someone who has slid so far into despair that they exist, feeding their addictions, just to keep breathing each day.

Not everyone who experiences sexual abuse becomes an addict, but as Dr. Matè points out, those with whom he worked, struggling with addiction, were almost without exception people who had been sexually abused. Brain chemistry is altered, creating vulnerability to seek a substance or behavior that soothes pain.

Addictive behavior can be subtle, but no less painful, whether it is about drugs, food or behavior. Anything we do obsessively, despite negative consequences on our life, can become an addiction.

The wounds of invasion dehumanize most when we are sensitive young children. Children don't know what sex is, but they do know when someone is hurting them.

So why do we continue to turn away from the ugliness of stolen innocence? We may not want to see it, but we can recognize the sorrow of sexual abuse in someone's eyes if we pay attention. Especially when it happens in early childhood, sexual abuse wounds are so deep that many people never recover and instead turn to drugs, alcohol, or compulsive, addictive behaviors, in attempts to ease the pain...

I didn't understand what was going on in the house where I grew up. I could feel danger and something dark and dense that was like a choking smoke in the air. I felt I'd done something wrong, though I could never figure out what it was. I just felt bad all the time, waiting for punishment, with no idea why.

I remember clearly the twisting of my psyche as I learned to ignore what hurt, and I didn't feel good, while clueless adults seemed to be just fine with it all. They smiled at me, told me I was a "good girl" and was "taking care of my dad." I thought he was supposed to take care of me...It was very confusing.

My brother must have been even more confused, because he was the one being sexually abused by our dad. But he couldn't talk about it, because a kid doesn't even know how to describe what is happening. He and I couldn't talk about it either, but he knew that I knew and I knew that he knew I knew...

We both pushed the pain down where no one else would see it, so that we could function semi-normally. The price we paid was losing the connection with our sense of knowing what is true and what is a lie.

I was just seven or so when I began washing the blood from his underwear, as if that could rinse away the awful truth of what was happening. Without being told to do so, I pulled the soiled ones from the pile at the bottom of our basement stairs, where everyone threw their dirty clothes. And all I knew for sure was that if I didn't put his clothes in the ringer washer and hang them on the line to dry, no one else would. I also knew not to ask any questions.

As a teen, after I left home at age thirteen, I experienced sexual abuse on the street. My first sexual experience was three days of rape in an abandoned house. I didn't know what intimacy was supposed to be like, though my well-honed ability to shut off my emotions came in handy then.

I thought I had to let people use my body to get what I wanted. I traded myself for food, for a place to sleep and, mostly, in the hope of seeing in another's eyes that I was worthy and good. I'd look, but I rarely saw anything like that...

As Matè says, "All addiction is an adaptation to pain." Whatever substance or behavior boosts the production of the neurotransmitters we've been lacking, then that is what we reach for to soothe ourselves.

Gabor also wisely observes, "It almost works," so we keep doing it over and over again...until something breaks the cycle. And if the cycle can break, for even a short time, the light can get in to where we are broken.

Like the Leonard Cohen song says, "There's a crack, a crack in everything. That's how the light gets in."

Nothing and no one is beyond redemption.

Don't Waste It

Life can be difficult and when it is we may be able to choose what we do with what life is handing us. For me, I know that my choices could have been much less clear and more difficult were it not for things like the light color of my skin and being born in a peaceful country, which made many things easier for me.

Choice is also constrained by what is going on in our environment and what other types of privilege and advantage we may or may not have. Choice is not just a matter of choosing.

We can rage against what is, and we can also use the difficulties we experience to gain insight and deepen our compassion. This doesn't mean we can't work for change and actively help others, only that the bumps along the way can inform us how to proceed, if we only slow down and give our precious time and attention to what is most clear.

When I was eighteen I lived in a communal house with a bunch of Bhagwan Shree Rajneesh devotees, who wore orange clothes and believed in love and freedom. I'd been homeless and wandering and they sort of took me in like a surrogate family.

Shortly after I started living there, I came down with a bad case of Hepatitis A. My liver was swollen and I was jaundiced. I felt like a flattened balloon. Because I was such an extreme case, the doctor brought in med students to observe and then advised me to rest for at least a couple of months in bed, with no activity and only very light food.

I went back home to the Rajneesh house and told them I was sick and needed to just do nothing. The doctor said I should even limit speaking or sitting up until I felt strong again, so I was promptly sent to the upstairs room for my extended rest time. Seeing they had a sick kid on their hands, the group took care of me, bringing me soup, ginger ale and water, and encouraging me to only get up to go to the bathroom.

One day one of the older women in the house sat on the edge of my bed and held my hand. "You know Sweetie," she said, "you are sick right now and you will have to be very still and quiet for a long time. This is an opportunity for you to go inside and learn what it is to be silent. I want to see you pay attention to this. Don't waste it."

I guess I was in a vulnerable enough state that I understood what she meant, so the next three months for me were spent laying there breathing, sleeping and hovering in states between sleep and waking. At times I slept for twenty-four hours or more, then I'd wake up not knowing what day it was, or even who I was.

I could watch myself falling asleep, noticing the last fragments of me disappearing into the nothingness of slumber. I had nothing else to do but pay attention to the delicacy of my consciousness. It was a very special time.

Gradually, I began to feel stronger and I woke up one day hungry for the first time in months. It was springtime! Birds cheeped outside my window, the air was sweet with cherry blossoms and I felt like dancing. It had been January when I got sick; now it was early April and I'd slept right through the winter. I felt alive and ready to live a new life.

I will never forget that time – the kindness of the people and the wisdom of my friend who taught me one of the most valuable lessons about using adversity as an ally to learn from. A month after feeling recovered from my illness I was invited to work on The Ranch in Oregon, a whole new adventure and a whole new start for me.

The lesson and the blessing will always be with me, though: when things are difficult, I still need to remind myself at times that this too will pass. Don't waste it.

Is It Safe?

In the 1970s suspense thriller, *Marathon Man*, Dustin Hoffman finds himself held hostage by the sinister Dr. Szell, who terrorizes Hoffman with an assortment of pointy dental tools, continuously asking, "Is It Safe?"

We cringed, watching with one eye closed, fingers clawed on our jawlines in horror, while marveling at Hoffman's calm answers to the repeated question, "Is it safe?" Yet there was no right answer.

How can we know if it is safe? And where is safe for us? Is safety a time or a place or is it a feeling that can exist even in the midst of danger?

Is it possible to find a safe and peaceful place of refuge, even when all around us feels chaotic? And if so, where might that safe place be?

When I was very young and my mom left, we were devastated. My dad thought she'd come back, because she always had, but months went by and she never returned. A kid thinks it's their fault and then blocks that out too, because it's too big a weight to carry.

When she grabbed us off the street one afternoon and took us across town on a bus to her basement suite, we stayed there for what seemed like such a very short time to me, though years later my dad would say it was a couple of weeks we were with her. I thought about my dad then, but pushed that from my mind, too. I felt guilty, never knowing what would happen next.

One day while he was driving cab, our dad found us by accident, while we played in the yard. There he was at the top of the street, standing by his car, his silhouette backlit by the sun, arms wide, calling us. My brother ran and I froze, too confused to know what to do. There was no good choice between running to him and leaving her.

I must have run, though, because I was in the car with my dad and brother, not knowing how I got there. Then she was gone from my life for nine years.

I didn't know it then, but these particular events influenced my decision-making processes for decades. I had such trouble knowing how to make the simplest choices and more difficult, important ones were so excruciatingly confusing that I became overwhelmed, shut down and usually made a bad choice that hurt me.

I never felt safe.

I believed I was not capable of knowing what to do or what not to do. It was a belief, based on fear and uncertainty, based on my early childhood experience of being forced to make an impossible decision.

In our world we feel great uncertainty and then we feel fear about being uncertain. Yet uncertainty is all we have ever really had. None of us know what the future holds. It's just that in our fear we can make a lot of assumptions and some of our assumptions can lead to unwise choices.

Even in moments when we are being harmed and threatened, we may still find ways to be in touch with a place inside, where we are sovereign and safe. The key lies in our willingness to be aware of our feelings throughout the day, practicing this awareness when we feel safe and relaxed, so we can remember the feeling and use it as a touchstone to center and ground us when we are afraid. We can sit here now and see if we can feel our seat on the chair, our hands, our breath…If we can get in touch with it and remember how safe feels, we can use this feeling whenever we need to feel safe.

We can change the habit from remembering each fearful thing to remembering safety. Practice feeling the feeling of safety, until it's as familiar as fear.

Our desire for safety is legitimate and sane. And ultimately, we want safety because we want peace. So is peace the common denominator of all that's desired in the world? If I have more money, more fame, more power…I will have…everything…and that will give me…peace? Maybe all of our striving is out of the hope that in the end we will finally have peace.

Even tyrants want peace and since they can't get in touch with peace inside, they demand from the world what they think will lead to, at last, having what they want.

And in a way, we're all tyrants. It's a matter of degree, how rigidly we cling to our preferences and opinions. We want what we want and we want it Right Now!

But don't take my word for it. Just try it, right now. Ask yourself: is it safe? Even a little bit? Use that. Remember that. Look for the peace and be that.

Our world might depend on you.

Kathy

Kathy and I met in grade six, when we were both about twelve years old. She was so different from the rest of us, with her dark straight hair, hawkish nose and brown eyes, kind of like a young Cher. She also looked tough and sad when she walked into our classroom. "You can sit here," I said, gesturing to the empty desk across the row from mine. Without a word, she strode over, sat down and flashed me a crooked smile. We were instant friends.

Kathy and her mother moved to Vancouver from rural Saskatchewan, where, she told me, "My mom got pregnant from my dad, who is Indian, and he went to jail so my mom took me away and married my new dad, Carl, when we came here. Carl is a banker and I live in a nice house now with my own room. My mom is happy. I'm a half breed. Want to come to my house after school?"

We became inseparable, hanging out almost every day, lying on the floor in her family's den, singing at the top of our lungs to Carol King, Shawn Philips and Carly Simon on the stereo. We played guitar together, laughed and talked about boys. I didn't know anything about boys, but Kathy knew all kinds of things.

In Saskatchewan, Kathy had already kissed boys and let them feel her up, which I could understand, because compared to my little "strawbs" as the boys called my strawberry-sized breasts, Kathy had peaches, which she flaunted in low cut tops, much to delight of her juvenile *and* adult audiences…

I spent a lot of time at Kath's house. Her parents didn't seem to mind me and didn't seem to think I was a bad influence on their daughter. Actually, it was the other way around for once. I was so happy that Kath was allowed over to my house after school, where she didn't even care that my dad and brother ogled her full figure as she wiggled up to my room, and we spent hours giggling and playing my Beatles Red Album over and over.

I admired the fact that Kath didn't care when people stared at her boobs. In fact, she was so used to the attention that she just shined it on whenever someone looked at her, smiling and looking like she enjoyed it. No one ever looked at me the way they looked at her. I thought Kathy was magic.

On weekends Kathy always wanted us to hitchhike, right in front of her parents' house on South East Marine Drive in Vancouver. We'd stand there in the rain with our thumbs out, taking rides from carloads of guys, who'd give us cigarettes, pot and beer.

She wasn't afraid of anything and sometimes Kathy would end up necking in the backseat with one of them, then I'd get scared when they tried to kiss me too. Amazingly, we always seemed to get away safely, then we'd fall over laughing together. Kathy was so bad and so much fun.

We got really drunk at a party once, having each gotten a twenty-sixer of vodka from a local pervert, who went to the liquor store for us. We went to a teeny bopper party where the parents were gone for the evening and there I must have drank the whole bottle of booze, mostly mixed with cream soda with some Kentucky Fried Chicken as a chaser.

I don't remember anything, but Kath said I puked my guts out and then ran all the way home in my underwear. I woke up the next morning feeling dreadful, looking in the mirror at my fat lip and chipped front tooth and wondering if my dad knew I'd been drunk. He didn't speak to me for a week, so I was pretty sure he did know.

Even after that, Kath's parents still let me come over and her dad even made a joke about it a couple of days later when both Kathy and I were still feeling a bit green around the gills. "How would you girls like a nice vodka and orange juice?" he laughed. It still makes me queasy just thinking about that epic hangover.

We took pills, too, another bad thing Kath introduced me to. Taking twenty Gravol tablets is not something I recommend to anyone. It just makes you feel like shit, but we did it anyhow and I'm not sure why. I did a lot of things with Kathy that I never felt right about, but because it was with her, it kind of made it okay. I never wanted to say no to her. I was afraid to lose her friendship.

A few years after I left home, Kathy also left home and moved in with a guy in Richmond. He was creepy and she was so devoted to him. I didn't get it. One time she invited me to their place and as soon as she left the room he tried to grope me and kiss me. I was so grossed out I left and I didn't see Kath for years after that.

The next time I saw Kath she was living back at her parents' house and was getting married to some guy she'd met. Meanwhile, she was having sex with another guy the night before her wedding day, like it was no big deal.

She told me about the whole thing, like we were twelve-year-old brats, telling stories about boys. She chatted away about sneaking out last night and screwing what's his name, like it was nothing, while she laughed, sitting on the side of the tub, shaving her legs.

A beautiful wedding gown lay on the bed, ready for her to wear. My stomach turned as I looked outside at her parents' yard and all the people gathering for the wedding. The place was full of flowers and tables were set with linen tablecloths; the sun was shining, everyone was wearing nice clothes, looking happy and excited.

"But Kath, you're getting married today. Don't you love the guy you're marrying?"

"Yeah, but that'll never last and I don't give a shit," she said.

"Then don't marry him!" I yelled at her and she looked at me, hurt and shocked.

"Wow," she said. "You've changed."

I guess I had changed, or maybe I just started figuring out who I was without her. Kathy and I had bonded in our unspoken childhood loss and trauma, both of us acting out what we couldn't even have voiced at the time. Over the years, I'd received help and support from my social worker and others, which I doubt Kathy had. And so we'd grown apart, going our separate ways, no longer two kids with the same types of struggles. I missed Kath, but it seemed now that too much had happened to us both to be able to pick up where we'd left off and be friends again.

I left that day, before the wedding started and walking to the bus stop, not even knowing where I was going, I'd never felt so alone.

SAFETY

Depending on who you are and what your circumstances are, safety can mean different things. To someone with millions of dollars, safety may mean knowing their money is secure and, therefore, available to be used to buy what they need and desire. To a woman living on the streets, safety may mean a place to sleep where it's quiet and she can't be seen by predators. Neither of these people may actually feel a sense of safety, though they may attempt to set up situations where it feels at least safe to relax for a bit. Our feeling of safety is definitely subjective and strongly influenced by past experience.

I lived my teen years without a stable home and stayed in many different places growing up. It was easy for me to become anxious when I had to move or even if I had to travel, which felt like leaving everything behind once again. Much later, when I moved to the U.S. from Canada, I was so anxious that my immune system went into a tailspin and it took me months to recover. I didn't feel healthy again until I started feeling safer and more familiar in my new environment.

And I keep wondering, what would it take for me to feel safe? Are we ever really safe, though? Is safety about environment or something deeper? I didn't even know what I was afraid of, other than the unknown, and not knowing what would come next had me feeling and acting defensive. Then, as I settled in, I saw that I could bit-by-bit let go of my wall of defense and I started to feel safer. It seems paradoxical to think that dropping my defenses might have been a part of feeling safe.

Am I afraid of something outside of me? Immediately I answer with, "Of course!" But am I also afraid of my own fear? That is, in fact, what I am most afraid of. And yet, even my fear wants relief. It is weary, burdened and burdensome.

Is it possible to be open to the possibility of change, while at the same time standing up for who we are and what we believe is right? Does less defense mean less offense? Then will there be less to be afraid of? I don't know, but I'll keep looking for the answers.

My Brother

I'd like to have been able to write that I'd just seen my brother Michael, that we had a happy reunion after so many years, that I felt good being connected with him. But none of that's true. I haven't seen him in about nine years and that's been intentional.

Michael and I grew up together. We're four years apart. I wish I could feel about him the way I figure other people with big brothers feel – loved, doted on, protected…but none of that's true either. Lately though, I've started to feel something other than dread at the thought of seeing him again.

For many years I'd seen him off and on. When Mom was living in Vancouver's West End, and Nora was visiting, Mom would insist on a contrived and bizarre "normalcy" of having her three remaining children over for dinner in her cramped apartment as often as possible.

I'd sit there at the table, holding my breath, resisting the urge to bolt, trying to not say anything to ruffle anyone's feathers, just counting the minutes till I could go outside and breathe again. Nice family dinner. Yes, nice and normal alright.

My brother lives his small, isolated life within a few blocks each day. He's never worked, and is on permanent disability due to the psychic damage of his youth. I left home when I was thirteen and he was sixteen. I escaped, but he didn't and I hate to think of what it was like for him after I was gone and there was no barrier between him and our dad.

Me at my brother Michael

Many years after they divorced, when I was about fifteen, Mom sued our dad for half the house, which she hadn't received when they split. My dad had to sell the house, he and Michael parted ways and Michael had to find his own place to live, finally being free to start a new life. Michael had never lived on his own and was quite helpless, I think, so thanks to social services, he has a roof over his head and a bit of welfare money to buy food. He goes to the library a lot and reads. I imagine that it's warm there and he gets to feel part of a society that only values you if you look like them. He doesn't look like the throngs of hipsters walking Vancouver's streets.

He lopes down sidewalks, wearing a heavy coat all year round, icy blue eyes darting here and there, looking out for danger. He is just another one of Vancouver's downtown freaks and as his only real claim to fame, I think he sort of revels in it.

I almost visited Michael when I was in Vancouver last time. I went to his door and rang the buzzer. I'd plucked up my courage on the train ride there and had a $50 bill wadded in my hand for him. Surprisingly, as I stood there, trying his room bell one last time, I didn't remember my brother sitting on my chest, punching me in the face when I was a kid. That usually happened right after he had been beaten. As the blows landed, I don't know who was crying more, him or me…but I wasn't thinking of that.

Instead, standing in the rain at his door, I had a memory of us doing what we did most rainy Sundays after church. As the rain poured on our street and into the gutters, we'd race "boats" made of sticks, all the way down the block, laughing, playing, soaking wet. I could feel him holding my hand as we walked back up the hill for another round of boat races, just like a big brother would do…I remember the sense of goodness and fun when it was just us two, being kids.

And I remembered how, as a three year old toddler, I'd squish beside him on the couch, watching him read Green Eggs and Ham. "You can read, too," he'd tell me. "Look, this word is 'the' and whenever you see this word, just say 'the.' And this word is 'green' and this one is 'ham' "…and in this way, he taught me, so patiently, like a big brother, how to read.

The good memories are resurfacing as I heal. And I'm not filled with fear and dread at the thought of seeing my brother anymore. He wasn't home today, so I'll try again, another time.

Empty

Emotions can often directly correspond with feelings in our bodies. We can feel "heavy-hearted" emotionally and physically have that same type of sensation, experienced as oppressive weight on our chest. We can feel "spaced out" and "not grounded" and literally have a light-headed sense of equilibrium.

For me, the feeling I had for many years was "emptiness." Around the time I was thirteen and left home, I can remember feeling empty. It's hard to explain the exact feeling but it was as though I had no top and no bottom, just a feeling of space with no walls, no boundaries, just empty, vast desolation.

It was also around that age that I stopped eating. I went from eating little, to eating almost nothing. My friend Rochelle called me a "tea waif" because tea was all I'd have some days. If I ate, I'd do it around other people so they'd think I was "normal." But when I was alone, I ate nothing.

The feeling of eating nothing, of being empty, was somehow comforting to me because my emotions felt like my body did, empty. Being empty physically was my touchstone for how I felt emotionally. I felt oddly safe when I was empty. Emptiness was something very familiar to me.

Anorexia is a complex disease and, from what I've read, I wasn't the classical type of anorexic young woman. I knew I was thin and I didn't have a distorted image of how I looked, but not eating was an obsession, an addiction, which was slowly killing me.

By the time I was fifteen, my menstrual cycles stopped, my hair was falling out, I was cold all the time and I ached all over. Doctors told me to eat protein and drink milk. I would rather have died than take their advice.

I'd missed most of grade eight, missed all of grade nine and I went back to school for most of grade ten, which was when something started to shift for me. Being around more kids my age got me out of feeling empty so much of the time.

I excelled in some subjects, like English, Drama and Phys Ed, and the empty spot in me started to fill in a comfortable, not so scary, sort of way. I even started eating a bit more and after another year or so, my menstrual cycles returned and I was on the road to recovery. I also had a great social worker who never stopped believing in me. Slowly I felt more whole.

I've learned that my empty feeling came from the sense of being invisible when I was a child. Things no child should have to witness were said and done in my presence as if I wasn't there and my only way to cope was to try to disappear so I didn't have to feel pain. Emptiness controlled me and I was afraid of the power it had over me.

Time and understanding are healing me and now emptiness means something different than the vacant, barren sense of loss I felt. I'm no longer afraid of the bottomless pit of despair. It's now just a small puddle. And when I sit silently and still every morning, the feeling of being empty "like the hollow bamboo" is precisely what helps me to let go and release into nothingness. Emptiness has become my friend.

TRANSFORMATION
——— THROUGH TRAUMA ———

Post-traumatic stress is not a disorder. Being traumatically stressed is a normal response when something unimaginable happens to you. This aftermath of trauma does not have to be pathological. The "dis-order" brews up when the trauma has not been integrated, discharged and understood. What we learn from the trauma we experience is part of growth, which can hold the potential for profound realization, if we can be open to trying something new.

Finding a way to see and feel a different perspective in the midst of reoccurring, daily trauma requires even more strength to do so within the experience of adversity. Even though I remember the feeling of being trapped in dangerous environments and circumstances and how it seemed there was no perspective, I have the luxury now of not having to live that way.

I do though, remember the pain and isolation of believing I would always feel alone, so I keep trying to step back and look at all of my life, to see what insight I can gain from it, especially from the difficult parts.

Many difficult experiences in life can alter perceptions and shape how we continue to live, though difficulties do not have to irreparably damage us. Having a skilled therapist to talk to, who can listen and reflect insights back, can be very helpful, though even without access to professional help, we can still use self-care skills, like journaling and breathing exercises, to feel more peaceful and grounded.

Trauma continues to hurt us because we have not learned how to process and allow all experiences to become part of who we are. We cannot, after all, change the past, but we can discover how even the hardest things hold pearls of wisdom, rather than shutting down and becoming numb. Learning how to use self-care in order to check in, feel and then sensitively respond to our own needs, is how we start to break the cycles of avoiding and numbing feelings.

When we try to numb ourselves to stop painful memories and feelings, we also block joy. It's not possible to selectively numb, only choosing to block out what hurts. Our sensitivity, happiness and joy get blocked out, too.

Integration is a delicate art we can cultivate to help us to see that we are continuously changed by life. Then we can find what is beyond the pain.

Bitch

I don't know any woman who hasn't been called bitch, me included. But what does it mean and why is this label historically thought of as negative? Or is it?

Before I left home, when we were both thirteen, I was at my friend Kathy's house after school. We were listening to Carol King on the record player, when her mother, Vivian, came in, telling Kathy she had to do her homework and clean her room.

"What a bitch," Kathy sighed, as her mom closed the door. It wasn't the first time I'd heard Kathy say the "B" word about her mom, but it still shocked me and made me feel sad and all crumpled inside.

I longed for a mother in my life to care about my room being clean, or whether my homework was done, having "lost" mine at age three when my parents were divorced and my dad got a bogus and cruel restraining order to keep her from visiting my brother and me.

In spite of coming from a "good home," Kathy was much more reckless and "bad" than I was and when Kathy's mother overheard us swearing and giggling about boys one afternoon, she chastised us and told me I had to go home.

"Vivian is such a bitch. This is bullshit," Kathy sighed, rolling her eyes. "You better go. I'll see you tomorrow."

"Yeah, okay" I said, starting to gather my jacket and shoes.

I felt sad, not just about disappointing Kathy's mother, but also because I'd appeared stupid and powerless in front of Kathy. I looked up to her as a sister and I liked being at her house, where there were two responsible adults and it was clean and not crazy and filthy like my house. I was invited often for dinner and stayed there on most weekends, just like part of the family.

When Carl and Vivian went boating in the summer, Kath and I came along, riding on the bow, our legs dangling, hair blowing in the wind, arms wrapped around each other.

Somewhere in the back of my mind I believed it was just a matter of time before Vivian and her banker husband Carl would ask me to move in and live there forever.

So I really didn't want to go home to my smelly, stupid house. I wanted to stay there with Kathy and her parents. I wanted Kathy to admire me, to look up to me. I wanted to be able to feel like I was accepted, even if I wasn't perfect, and for her mother to tell me to brush my teeth and clean my room…

Feeling torn between wanting to be a "good daughter" to Kathy's parents and being someone Kathy would respect for not "putting up with bullshit," I saw my chance to impress her with my coolness and let her mom know I was not to be trifled with. Maybe now Kathy would stand up for me and tell her mom that she wanted me to stay. They would both respect me more…

"Vivian you are such a bitch," I said, just loud enough for both Kathy and her mom to hear. Stomping down the stairs and flipping my feathered bangs, I was confident that Kathy would not only agree with me, but I was sure she would be proud that I, too, could speak my mind.

Strutting out, I glanced back defiantly, expecting a sly smile of approval from Kathy but instead there were daggers in her eyes.

"Don't you ever call my mom a bitch!" she hissed. The door slammed hard and it was a long walk home.

I learned the lesson then and many times afterwards, that the word bitch is personal and it matters who says it. If you are "my bitch" I can call you that, but as soon as someone else calls you bitch, then we have a problem.

I dated a guy years ago who often used the word bitch when talking about women. "I hope you're not a bitch," he said to me one day. "I can't stand bitches."

"Oh no, I don't think I'm a bitch," I told him hopefully. "I just try to get along with everyone."

It took a while for me to realize that what he'd meant by the word bitch was a woman who didn't agree with him or bow to his wishes.

And I was a bitch because I didn't agree, didn't do what I was told, didn't conform. In other words, I'm someone who tries to stand up for myself and others when circumstances are unfair, hurtful and mean.

Soon, he was calling me "bitch." At first the word stung, but then I saw how being a bitch was my way to freedom and I left the relationship.

Around that same time, I was taking care of my dying mom, a self-proclaimed bitch, who was "too old to take shit anymore." We had a rough three years before she died, with her slinging insults at me every time I visited her in the nursing home. Mom was so angry and frustrated at being incapacitated that she lashed out at everyone, especially me.

I was the only visitor she had, coming faithfully to see her, day after day and enduring her emotional outbursts. I tried to be stoic but I was hurt, feeling beaten down by her treatment of me. After many months of her verbal abuse, one day I stepped away from her bedside and for the first time I let her know her behavior was not acceptable, then she hurled the word at me:

"Fucking bitch!" she screamed as I walked out.

My eighty-seven-year-old mom could still swear like a sailor. I kind of felt proud of her, plus I saw how scared she was and how she must have felt very alone and abandoned. There was no way I was giving up on loving her.

Poor mom.

I took a deep breath and said, "I'll be back tomorrow. I love you."

And I did come back, because bitches stick together.

—— LABELS ——

Some people don't have clean clothes or combed hair. Maybe they smell strongly, their hands are grimy, their shoes old and worn. And if you look closely, there's a deep weariness in their eyes and lines on their faces.

Many affluent people don't understand what it's like to be poor, without a place to live and so they slap a label on those who look like this, lumping them all in one homogenous category. The label has become "the homeless," like they are some other species of human.

And when a label has been stuck on someone, it's easier for a bunch of other labels to stick to the same place: Lazy, crazy, drug addict, alcoholic, deadbeat, criminal…It's as if once it is decided somebody is one of "the homeless," they are in danger of falling into a subgroup of "outcast." It's easier to categorize people than to care about someone individually, as a person in pain.

When I catch myself labeling people, I don't feel right about it. The more I notice the labels I try to pass off as some sort of "truth," the more I see how labels separate us from one another: man, woman, black, white, Democrat, Republican, gay, straight, rich, poor, homeless or...People who live where they feel safe, are not discriminated against and, most of all, are considered part of a society, rather than outcasts from it...

The consequence of a simple label on a person can be devastating.

I grew up with labels put on me, like: poor, smelly, loud, stupid, ugly, pretty, slut and bitch, to name a few... I internalized those labels, believing them, building on them, making even more of myself shrink to fit into one small category. I'm still shaking off what was imposed on me and I am still uncovering old beliefs that stuck, too. Those labels never were who I am.

The only thing a label does is make it more convenient for us to categorize and form opinions based on where we believe things fit. Labels can be useful for things.

But labels are not for people.

Dancer

Like many little girls, I dreamed of being a ballerina, but that was not something our family ever dreamed of for me. If I ever brought it up, "Daddy, I could be a ballerina. Watch me – I could do that!" I was met with a wagging finger and disdainful look. "That's silly. Stop dancing around like that. You're being vain!"

My dad and his religious doctrines saw my girlish exuberance as a dangerous thing which needed to be discouraged and controlled. But when their dreams are squelched harshly, a kid believes that they must have done something wrong.

I don't know where I got it from, because no one ever told me I was capable of anything special, but for as long as I can remember, dreams were the most important thing I had and for no good reason, I pretty much believed I could do anything.

I'd see other little girls being picked up after school by their parents in nice cars, taking them to their dance lessons. They had pink leotards and special shoes. One girl did Highland dance and wore a tartan skirt, with black slippers that laced up her legs.

I'd seen the Highland dancers at Kitsilano Showboat, where my dad took us on Friday nights in the summer. They looked so proud, delicately upright, sometimes dancing over swords placed on the ground. Just watching them dance made my legs and feet jump all around. I can do that! I can do that!

Many years passed, I left home at age thirteen and found myself living on the street, in and out of many foster homes, using my street smarts and survival skills to find wherever I could to stay and do whatever I could to eat. Even then, I'd dream at night about dancing on a stage, dressed in a fluffy pink skirt, on my toes in satin shoes, my hair all pulled up in an elegant bun. I floated and soared.

My social worker, John Turvey, whom I'd met at the first emergency shelter, always kept his eye on me and he asked me one day, "What's your dream? What do you want to do with your life?"

"That's easy," I said, "I want to be a dancer, but not like a stripper. I want to be a dancer like in the ballet!"

Seeing an opportunity to get me engaged in something, John jumped at it saying, "Okay then! We can get you enrolled in dance class up the street at The Paula Ross Academy, if you want. I know them and we can get it paid for."

"Wow."

Paula Ross was a modern dance school, specializing in the angular Martha Graham Modern style and Alvin Ailey type Jazz, in a rundown building on West Broadway in Vancouver, with windows all along the sidewalk. By this time I was back in school in grade ten and I took my dance very seriously, coming to classes several times a week.

Having dance in my life gave me an anchor, something to work for and care about, even when I didn't feel cared for.

It was weird, I guess, that even when I didn't have a proper place to live, I still went to school, had friends and went to dance classes, just like I was a normal teenager with a real home. But I loved the incongruity of it: Me, a dancer. I felt like dance gave me a secret life of grace and beauty that I just kind of stumbled into, just like a lot of things happened for me. It was a miracle.

I slept where I could, sometimes at my friend Rochelle's, sometimes with anyone I'd meet who'd buy me a meal. I had a few foster homes, but they usually only lasted a couple of weeks, for various reasons. Sometimes one of the adults (or even another kid) would try to sexually abuse me, or there wasn't any food. At one of the foster homes, I never got a key, so I'd have to wait outside, sometimes for hours for them to come home. So, many times the foster care was worse than nothing, so I'd leave and be out on my own again. I'd just wander, sleep during long bus rides or even find an unlocked car to crawl into…

Those were times I'd fall off the radar and get swept up in some messy sex or drug situation with bad people and I'd miss weeks of classes. "Where have you been?" Paula would demand when I'd stroll back to class in my shabby, torn tights.

"Sorry, Paula. I will try to not miss class."

"You'd better not!" she'd growl, but always with a glint in her eye, like she knew more about me than I'd ever shown her.

Paula told a couple of us younger girls that we should be going to ballet classes to "improve your lines and get ready to perform with the company." I was thrilled beyond words and after talking to my social worker, who said that could be paid for too, so I was permitted to attend classes at The Royal Academy of Ballet!

We had to wear perfect pink tights of a certain shade, a black one-piece leotard and little pink ballet slippers, with our hair in a tight bun and no old sweater sleeves on our legs, as had been my Flashdance kind of style at Paula Ross. Amanda, the other girl who came with me, and I tried not to laugh or roll our eyes at the snobby girls who somehow knew we were not one of them. We tried to behave and we both worked really hard.

We kept going to Paula's classes, too, being praised for how our "lines" were improving, while still going to the Academy for Ballet. Amanda and I were both learning to dance on pointe shoes now, which wasn't nearly as hard as I thought it might be. Mainly, you just had to hold in your stomach and think "up, like a string is tied to the top of your head" as the Academy teacher would keep saying as she played the piano for our classes. "Pinch pennies!" she'd tell us all the time, which meant to squeeze your butt cheeks really tightly together, as if you were holding a penny there.

Amanda and I were allowed to do some performances with the company and if I'd continued, I think I could have really gone somewhere with dance. As it was, I was pulled back to the street and then I moved to a commune in Oregon shortly after that, following another surrogate family, trying to find a home.

Dance was an important part of my growing up – learning how to take instruction and work towards a goal – and without it as a focus, I would certainly have been worse off.

I learned that one small dream can become a reality and that makes anything possible.

———— BEING "RIGHT" ————

Oh yes. We love to be "right," but what is that all about? The compulsion to come off as "right" can be ingrained in our personality, but as with all things, we see clearer when we start to dissect it.

Sure, we want to look intelligent and together, but is this why we defend our opinions so rabidly? Do we really think we look so great when we are tearing someone a new one because they don't agree with us? Maybe trying to look "right" all the time is just a transparent attempt to hide the root of our self-righteousness: fear.

It's pretty easy to see that we equate "rightness" with safety. When we are afraid, even if it's unconscious, we think that when we have the "right" information, we will be safe. The urge to show we are "right" is a maladaptive survival mechanism. "Righteous rightness" is a habit that doesn't work. We still feel scared, so we try harder to be "right" the next time.

We humans are funny. We want to connect with one another and there are times we do this brilliantly and times we fail utterly. Maybe the transcendent quality to wanting to be "right" is the desire to express what we believe to be true. Maybe we are even trying to say, I know what's "right" so you can trust me...

I don't know. Gee, it feels good to say that.

My Gay Boyfriends

Grade ten was pretty wild. I got off the street and into foster care for the beginning of it, started dance lessons, met new friends at school and even moved in with Mom for a few weeks. I had two great "boyfriends," too: Marcus and Bruce.

My early morning job was peeling carrots at a hippie health food store. Sometimes I'd disappear and miss a few weeks, but they were always happy to have my help if I showed up to get that two-hundred pound pile of carrots peeled and ground up for the juice press.

Curtis, the store owner, was a bit nuts, bug-eyed and always talking about how he was God's gift to womankind. I loved his fun brother Marcus, though, and we became good friends.

Marcus rode a big Kawasaki nine hundred, "bored out" to a thousand, and he had the coolest colorful leathers. He'd breeze into the store, talk to me and give me rides on his motorcycle all over town. He loved to push the bike to the limit and we'd fly down hills so fast that we were airborne, with me squealing on the back. Marcus took me to movies and the beach, cooked us dinners and never asked anything from me. I stayed at his West End apartment and we'd sit up all night talking like school girls.

Some of the kids at school teased me when he'd pick me up on his motorcycle after class, but I didn't care. I loved Marcus. He was the best!

Bruce owned a yogurt shop on Broadway, where a lot of kids stopped after school to get a cone. Marcus worked there, which is how I got to know Bruce. I met him at the shop one day after school and he smiled and started talking to me, which seemed to make Marcus uncomfortable. I didn't know it then, but Bruce and Marcus were lovers and there'd been some history of Bruce "stealing" Marcus's friends.

Not knowing any of their relationship drama, when Bruce suddenly invited me to the Royal Theatre that Friday night to see the Alvin Ailey Dance Company, I was thrilled. "I have two really good seats and I'd love to take you."

"I'd love to!" I said breathlessly, not even noticing that Marcus was hurt. It's not that I didn't care, but I was too self-absorbed to see anything but what I wanted.

The next day after school, a black limousine pulled up to where a group of my friends and I were standing. The driver's window rolled down and Bruce waved, "Hi there, would you like a lift?"

"Sure!" I said, climbing in the front seat beside him as my friends all stood there gawking.

"Where are you going?" Bruce asked.

"I just started living with my Mom on Oak and Fifteenth."

"Great! I'll take you there. But first can we go shopping?"

"What for?" I asked.

"I want to buy you something nice to wear when we go to the Royal on Friday."

"Wow! Really? Sure, let's go downtown!"

It was quite easy to find something pretty, because everything was pretty to me. I didn't own a dress and hadn't worn one in ages. I chose a long, light-blue one made of spandex with a halter tie at the back. It was slinky and made me feel like a movie star. Bruce said I looked so good he almost wished he wasn't gay and I took that as a compliment.

We went to the ballet that night and from then on, it was Bruce and me. Marcus stopped working at the yogurt shop and I hardly ever saw him. I tried calling him, too, but he didn't answer or return my calls.

Meanwhile, I'd been at Mom's place for a few weeks. It was the first time we'd lived together since I was three when she left. John, my social worker, kind of put pressure on her to take me in, because there were few good foster homes and I was just floating around on my own. I knew I "cramped her style" because Mom told me that, so I tried to be good and not bug her too much. She'd gotten used to being single and having a bratty fifteen-year-old around wasn't really what she wanted.

Then Bruce moved in across the hall! I couldn't believe it and even though I knew it would probably make things more complicated, I was delighted to have my new friend so close now. I even spent the night at Bruce's place sometimes and we'd giggle in bed, eating popcorn and watching TV. I thought it was funny that my Mom didn't know where I was and I was twenty feet away behind a door. I didn't think she cared anyhow, so I stayed there often and she never asked where I'd been.

My friend Rochelle sewed an evening gown for me for another date with Bruce, this time to the symphony. The dress was peach-colored, again with a halter neck and a low scoop back, down to my bum. It was gorgeous, Bruce said I was "a vision" in it and a few weeks later, we went to a Halloween party, her wearing the peach and me wearing the blue gown.

Rochelle thought it'd be funny if we pretended that we couldn't speak English, so we jabbered away all night in what we thought sounded like Swedish, giggling like idiots after everything we said.

It didn't seem like we were fooling anyone and the other girls at the party were looking pretty annoyed at the attention the boys were giving us so we hailed a cab and left for another party.

The last thing I remember is the two of us lying on the grass at the park by her house, laughing, then stumbling up the stairs where she lived with her mom and brother.

I had a party at Mom's because she was away visiting family on the East Coast. A bunch of kids stayed over, because there was lots of room and it was late by the time we all started passing out. Mom walked in unexpectedly the next morning to see a dozen or so kids sleeping in her bed and on the floor, my friend Markie playing her precious piano, with a beer bottle sitting next to him on the bench and a smoke hanging out of his mouth, which is what I think put her over the edge.

Markie stopped playing, everyone scattered out the windows like cockroaches and Mom booted me out right then and there. She threw my clothes out the window and locked the door and I was homeless again.

I told Bruce that afternoon, thinking he'd just tell me to come and live with him, but he didn't. He moved out the next month and I didn't see him as often. I stopped going to the yogurt shop and there were no more invites to the ballet, no more rides in the limo.

Marcus and I hung out a little, but our friendship was never the same. I guess I'd wrecked it, but I didn't know any better. I didn't know too much about loyalty and people's feelings and, besides, I kind of suspected that I was kind of being used for Bruce and Marcus to get at each other.

It made me sad and I missed my gay boyfriends. I think they might have missed me, too; not sure, but I hope so, just a little bit...

──── TRANSITION ────

Greek philosopher Heraclitus said, *"You could not step twice into the same river; for other waters are ever flowing on to you."*

His observation recognizes the ever-changing seasons and stages of life, whether it be summer turning to autumn, day to night, or sleep becoming awakening, the accumulation time's effect is indelible, and life just keeps flowing, even when we try to make it stay put. Cycles of the seasons repeat, but never in exactly the same way. Even our breathing is cyclical, continuing through our whole lives, yet we never take the same breath twice. We can try to hold on to feelings and experiences but, alas, it is not possible. Everything in life eventually transitions.

I've tried holding the moments of joy, peace and oneness in my life. But like sunlight on water, the moment cannot be held, cannot be stopped and cannot be reproduced at will. Even peace transitions in our world.

I guess this topic is on my heart today as autumn now takes the place of summer in the fall equinox. I've felt the transition for a while and I've welcomed the cooler nights of September, while also sadly saying goodbye to summer's carefree light and warmth. It seems that so many things in life are both difficult and beautiful at the same time.

Transitions are rich with many facets and dimensions, yet we never seem to "get used to" the flowing river of change, constant as it is...

PART II

POISONED BAIT AND PRECIOUS THINGS

The Ranch

Bhagwan Shree Rajneesh was a self-proclaimed Indian guru
popular in the 1970s and 80s with followers all over the world, each
wearing saffron colors and a sandalwood necklace with a black and
white photo of the guru. Bhagwan, also known as Osho, launched a
unique brand of human potential work, attracting an array of people
who saw his philosophy as a way to transcend what had held them
back in life, while celebrating freedom from society's conventions.

In the early 1980s, Bhagwan decided to move from his ashram in
Poona, India to a newly purchased one-hundred-square-mile ranch in
central Oregon near the small town of Antelope. Many of his followers
from India and other places abroad came to Oregon with him and
began to build a community there. I was one of those people.

I kind of stumbled into the movement, mostly because the
sannyasins (as they called themselves) were friendly to me and let me
live in their big communal house when I was a homeless teen, sick
with hepatitis. I started wearing red all the time, got a necklace with
Bhagwan's picture on it and even got a new name: Deva Vasudha,
which means "divine earth."

We danced a lot, meditated a lot and I began long-distance running
with those in the house who'd been doing it for several months. I'd
run for miles and miles with my crazy red-clad friends, trotting down
the middle of the road in the pouring rain, laughing and yelling at
the tops of our lungs. I liked the idea of starting out new and fresh, so
being a "sannyasin," one who renounces the past, seemed like a good
idea at the time.

Initiates were being asked to come to The Ranch to work and I
was part of a group of the first few hundred who got to go there. We

worked twelve-hour days, seven days a week. I lived in a tent in the woods and we were fed at a large cafeteria three times a day. The food was really good, deluxe vegetarian hippie food, which suited me fine. We got one beer every day, free cigarettes if we wanted, our laundry was done for us and we were just generally like a bunch of horny teenagers, being cared for, as long as we worked seven days a week. It sounds weird, but I loved it.

Women were given a lot of responsibility because Bhagwan wanted it that way and as a nineteen-year-old girl I was given a construction crew to manage. I had no idea what to do with a construction crew, so a man experienced in construction was to be my advisor and he told me what to tell others to do. He'd explain to me what we were building and how it would be done and then he'd help me manage the crew, always deferring to my authority. Of course I loved this as well. What young woman wouldn't?

At the end of the workday we'd have dinner and then there was a disco every night that'd go until two. I went almost every night, dancing like mad to Stevie Wonder, until it was time to go to bed and then get up and do it all over again.

I worked on several big projects, one of which was building two thousand tent platforms, which would later be propped up into triangles, turning them into A-frame cottages. We set up a metal template for the two-by-six frames to drop into, then used nail guns to put them together. Next, the whole frame was lifted onto a platform, where plywood went down, chalk lines were snapped for the nails to go in and the next crew nailed down the plywood boards. All this happened in a joyful, dancelike way, to the loud music of Steely Dan blasting from truck speakers.

Bhagwan drove by every day while we worked, in one of his many Rolls Royces, and waved at us. That was about all I saw of him, besides a few darshans, where he'd sit in a chair, smiling and clapping his hands, while we danced wildly to loud Indian music.

I didn't really care about the "guru" aspect of it all, because for me it was all about being with a surrogate family and living in a community. That was the biggest thing for me. I felt safe and respected there and I never wanted to leave.

But I did have to leave after about a year, when my time for being in the U.S. as a foreigner was up. Arriving back in Vancouver to start a new life, I cried for a bit then got on with things, moving in with my friend Rochelle and baby Ryan.

Within a few weeks, I'd dropped all my red clothes and mala and began wearing jeans, cowboy boots and Harley Davidson tee shirts, and going back to using my old name. I'd become pretty resilient with all I'd experienced. It was good for me.

The Ranch was a wild ride, with a lot of amazing memories. I have a lot more stories to tell and even though living on The Ranch wasn't what most people would wish for their daughters, it was the right timing for me and I thrived there.

I even cherish the name I was given, divine earth. It fit then and it still does.

—— POISONED BAIT ——

Sometimes something that looks or sounds good turns out to be not so good and can even be harmful, though, if we are mature, healthy and have good boundaries, we can usually gain enough perspective to make choices that protect our safety and well-being. But why is it that we can sometimes make decisions we might later regret?

In her provocative book, Women Who Run With the Wolves, *Clarissa Pinkola Estès celebrates women's wild nature with colorful reinterpretations of folk tales from many different cultures. One of the chapters is titled "Self Preservation: Identifying Leg Traps, Cages, and Poisoned Bait." This is the chapter I read over and over again when I got the book twenty years ago. And what I learned then about poisoned bait is still useful today.*

I see now all of the poisoned bait I followed and swallowed in my life, and how I made the decisions I did in those moments, based on either trying to run from or fight something. My nervous system, in fight or flight mode, dictated almost everything I did. Saying it's a "bad decision" is a simplification and judgment which misses the fact that even if the result was catastrophic, it seemed like a good idea at the time.

I was talking the other day with a friend who'd had early trauma in her life who said she "did a lot of crazy things" that were not just reckless, but frightening. I could relate, too, because as a young girl I regularly hitchhiked, taking poisoned bait by getting into cars and going places with people who did not have my best interests at heart.

I longed for almost anyone to care for me and settled for the attention of a compliment from someone who was enough "bait" to temporarily ease my pain and help me escape the belief that I was not lovable. But the bait was poisoned.

When we're tempted to reach outside of ourselves for relief from the pain, we don't usually know that's what we're doing. It seems like a good idea on some level, because we don't listen to something deeper that is frantically flashing the warning signals, which we ignore.

Following poisoned bait is not always dangerous, catastrophic and horrible. Much of the time we can learn what I call "cheap lessons," because not much is at stake, though the lesson is no less valuable if we pay attention. Those times when we do notice what's precious and not, what's important and not, what is nonnegotiable and what can be tossed, are the most important lessons of life and we learn them sometimes easily and sometimes the hard way.

But once we know what is true, we have no appetite for any type of bait and no bait is required for us to think and act clearly.

Clarity comes from the inside.

The Car

I kind of thought I could drive, way before I actually got behind the wheel. I'd seen my dad drive a million times and it looked stupidly simple. You just sit there and turn the wheel a bit, push the pedals now and then and relax. Seemed like something a kid could do easily.

His big blue '55 Cadillac Fleetwood was parked in front of our house and was never locked, so whenever I could, I'd open the heavy door and sit in the driver's seat, feeling the dip in the springs where my dad always sat, imagining what it'd be like to drive.

Later on, when I was in my early twenties and we were speaking again after years of little or no contact, my dad got an Oldsmobile Cutlass. My brother David, who, true to

My Dad's big blue '55 Cadillac Fleetwood

sleazy form, was a salesman at a local used car lot, talked my dad into buying one of the only cars he'd own that wasn't a beat up old Cadillac.

It was a big gold "sexy chick magnet," as David told my dad. I think that's what actually sealed the deal. Oldsmobiles were more "sexy" than Cadillacs. At least that's what David said.

I'm guessing that the hate David had for his father was only surpassed by the desperation to be loved by him. I wasn't there for my oldest brother's childhood, but I would bet he'd suffered the abuse and neglect that all of us had felt.

"Yeah dad, this is a real beauty. Listen to her purr. Those old Caddies are for weddings and funerals. This is a fun car, built for speed. You're gonna love it, Pops!"

I guess that was one of their rare father-and-son bonding moments. Father wanted to ease his mind of guilt and his son wanted some payback for all the years of abuse from his father. It wasn't nearly enough. Not even close. But it would have to do.

When my dad was ill with prostate cancer a couple of years later and he couldn't drive any longer, he passed the car on to me. I'd never owned a car, didn't have a license, but I drove it everywhere, loving the freedom of my new sexy gold Cutlass. I'd given my dad a

Magic horsey figurine

cheap horse figurine from Chinatown and he proudly displayed it on the dashboard. It was faded now and the tasseled mane wiggled as the car moved. I decided to leave it there and called it my "magic horsey" to protect me while I drove.

One day when I was trying to park it, the transmission just went out on me. The reverse gear was gone. I had to grab some strangers to help push it out of the parking spot and I soon learned how it was better to park going uphill, with no one behind, so I could just sort of roll backwards to get out. It was kind of ridiculous, but better than no car.

My dad eventually died and so did the car, which had started blowing noxious blue smoke and making grinding sounds.

I said goodbye to my dad at the funeral, while we all sang "The Old Rugged Cross." My brother David was piss drunk and raving in the back row. My sister, Nora, kept grabbing my arm, trying to whisper to me. I just felt numb.

Mom sat beside me, wiping her eyes, wearing a brightly flowered dress, snapping at me when I'd questioned her choice of outfits for the funeral: "Your father would have liked me in this dress. It would have made him smile."

And even though she and my dad had been acrimoniously divorced more than twenty years earlier, I had to admire her for being sentimental, making me wonder, as I had many times, how it would have been if they'd been able to work things out and stay together. I guess a kid of divorced parents always wonders such things...

My brother Michael sat apart from us, looking pale and silently staring forward at the coffin.

Had he dreamed of this day when his tormentor would be no more? Or did he also grieve for the childhood and the father he never had? I can imagine it was both of those things...

There was no Irish wake for Dalton Smith. We went to the cemetery, put him in the ground and everyone just left, or at least I just left without a word to anyone.

The Cutlass was waiting for me. I walked out of the graveyard and drove away in a cloud of stinky smoke, the radio blaring some dumb song. I pulled over and parked on a side street, unscrewed the nuts holding the license plates and put them in a nearby garbage can.

As an after-thought, I went back and grabbed the "magic horsey" from the dashboard, stuffed it in my pocket and started walking. (That little horsey is one of the few things I've managed to hang onto over the years; it sits on the shelf by the bathroom sink and somehow comforts me when I look at it.)

The gray sky and rain matched something silent and neutral in me. I had no coat and I was getting soaked. It was a few days before Christmas, I'd just buried my dad, dumped my first car and the emptiness felt good.

Your Voice

It's pretty common knowledge that when people are unconscious, in a coma or even near death, the last sense to go is hearing. I've been teaching this for many years in paramedic and first-aid courses and I feel strongly about behaving respectfully to the person, even if they are dying or dead. Saying the things anyone would want to hear in that state is a very important part of doing the job right.

I tell my students to keep talking to an unconscious patient, no matter what. I tell them to say something like, "You're going to be okay." It's good to use their name, too, if you can and say, "I'm here with you." To me, even if you're dying, hearing "You're going to be okay" can be a true statement, because even if we are dying, we can still be totally okay...

One rainy afternoon in November I was working on ambulance in Vancouver when we received the call for a pedestrian struck. With lights and sirens we quickly arrived at the scene, flanked by police and fire department for assistance. My heart sank as we got closer and I saw it was an elderly lady lying in a pool of blood coming from her head.

She'd been hit by a delivery truck when she tried to cross the street. As I knelt down on the wet road to hold her head still (serious head and facial injuries equal upper spinal injuries in a paramedic's world) a bystander was talking to my partner: "Yeah, she was thrown through the air about fifteen feet or so and she hasn't moved since."

I could see that she had an open head wound and, most importantly, her airway was going to need suctioning immediately. My partner was grabbing all our equipment, a firefighter was getting the scoop stretcher and spinal immobilization equipment ready and we soon got her out of the pouring rain and into the back of the ambulance, where two more firefighters joined me to help on the way to hospital.

It's a special kind of crazy to be flung around in the back of a speeding ambulance with lights and sirens going, but it's even more intense when your patient is in such critical shape. I suctioned her airway and alternately ventilated her with a bag-valve mask, while one of the firemen held a dressing on her gaping head wound.

I kept looking at the old lady and thinking of my mom. I kept talking to her, saying: "You're going to be just fine. We're taking care of you and we're going to the hospital now. You're going to be just fine…" I didn't believe she was "just fine" but it was what I'd have wanted to hear if I was in her place.

We got her in and stayed long enough for the emergency doctor to tell us, "I'm amazed she's still alive. She has a fractured pelvis, ribs, collapsed lung and that head injury is pretty bad. She's eighty-six, so it doesn't look good." Sad, but all in a day's work, I thought.

My shift ended, weeks went by and one day my unit chief asked me to call a patient's relative about a personal item. The relative turned out to be the son of the old woman hit by the truck and when I called him he said, "Yes, we wanted to inquire about my mother's dentures. It seems they were knocked out by the blow and we were wondering if by chance you'd seen them."

"Oh. No," I said, sure that the lady had passed on. "Does she still…need them?"

"Oh yes! She's doing well and at the ICU at Vancouver General."

I've got to see this, I thought.

Next shift we dropped a patient off at the emergency at VGH and I went up to the ICU to see if I could catch a glimpse of this miracle lady. There she was in one of the glass rooms, tubes and monitors attached. She was sitting up in bed, all bruised and stitched up on her head, but eating something and looking a lot better than I'd expected.

I tapped on her door. "Hi there, Ma'am. How are you today? You look like you are doing just fine."

She stopped, put down her spoon and looked hard at me. "I know you. You are the girl who helped me when I got in the accident, aren't you?" I was stunned.

"How did you know?" I asked, incredulous.

"Oh dear, I recognize your voice. Thank you."

INTUITION,
—— GUT AND HEART ——

We are born with basic survival information that *can instantly tell us how to be safe. We naturally rely on nervous-system cues, quite literally from our small intestines, which are richer in neuro-receptor circuits than even our brains. No wonder we call intuition "gut instinct."*

When I was a teen living on the street I had to keep my eyes open for threats. From growing up in a violent home environment, I developed strong intuition, so I knew when to get out of the way and run if I sensed a threat. Walking down the street, I could spot a predator from a mile away, and most times I'd go the other direction. My gut kept me safe, when I listened to it.

Intuition also informs us how to care and know deep ways to express love for one another. It's a different sort of intuition that seems to come from another place, the heart. I feel it, right in the center of my chest.

When my Mom was dying, my heart did all the talking to her at the end. There was no thinking of what to say, just a stream of love from my heart to hers, tying together all the threads between us, wanting to undo all she thought she'd done wrong, helping prepare her for her journey home. Gut and heart are integrated in love.

Rochelle

Rochelle and I met at an emergency shelter in Vancouver when we were both thirteen. I arrived there by squad car, when police had scooped me out of an abandoned house where I was being "groomed" for prostitution. The police blindfolded me and made me keep my head down in the back of the car. I didn't question or resist it at the time. I guess they didn't want me to know where they were taking me.

And when we arrived at the shelter, I didn't know where I was, only that it looked better than where I'd come from. One of the staff, John, walked out to greet me in his afro, a smile and lots of tattoos on his arms, speaking softly and telling me dinner was ready. He would later become my social worker and most stable influence during those chaotic teen years.

John Turvey[1], who'd been a biker-gang member and heroin addict, got clean and helped many people, starting the first needle exchange program in Vancouver's gritty Downtown Eastside and tirelessly advocating for anyone who needed help.

John stood by me through all of my ups and downs, doing his best to find suitable foster care for me, which often didn't work out. When there were no more options to house me, he and his girlfriend Petra took me into their own home for a summer, giving me a safe place to be.

My first night there, I had my own bed to sleep in, with crisp clean sheets, and Petra left a bowl of cherries and almonds on the bedside table to let me know I was welcome.

After that, I came home every night rather than staying out. And even if it was late, I had a key so I was able to creep in and quietly go to sleep on my own. With no one judging or threatening me, there was space for me to feel at home and that was very healing. I felt gratitude and respect for John and Petra and, gradually, I started feeling respect for myself.

[1]https://en.wikipedia.org/wiki/John_Turvey

Those couple of months of safety, peace and love in their home helped lay a foundation of stability in me and even though I was still on the streets and occasionally in foster care for a few more years, I had a different feeling about who I was and life gradually got better. I will never forget how much it meant to me to be accepted and welcomed.

At the shelter, Rochelle was the first kid I saw when I walked in and she smiled at me with braces on her teeth and big googly eyes. I loved her from then on and for many years we were inseparable.

The shelter was supposed to keep us safe and none of the ten or so kids could leave the house while we were there. It was kind of like prison, but the group home staff was really nice and they fed us well. Of course we got bored, so we did things like sniffing glue on the fire escape or getting contraband drugs like over-the-counter Gravol pills, which we'd all take by the handful to get a sort of "low high" that would last hours and make you feel like crap.

We both got out eventually and Rochelle moved back in with her mother and brother. I spent several more years in and out of foster care, on the streets and anywhere I could find to sleep. I went to a year or so of high school, then quit, hitchhiked to California, planted trees for the BC forestry service, picked fruit in the Okanogan, painted houses and joined a commune in central Oregon until I was politely told to go back to Canada or face immigration issues.

When I arrived at the bus depot I called Rochelle, who'd had a baby at age sixteen and was now living with her four-year-old son in Vancouver. "Can I come and live with you?"

"Yeah," she said, "come on over."

Rochelle got me a job at the restaurant where she worked, we partied every weekend, shopped and had a total renaissance of our crazy teen years, enjoying the eighties and having the time of our lives. Ryan was a happy little guy, always laughing, singing and keeping us on track enough to put food on the table and make a stable life for our little family. Those were the days, great days.

Rochelle got pregnant again, though, which put the brakes on our happy life and I didn't like the father much. He called her "Raw

Hell," which I thought was funny, but not coming from him. He was a tough heroin-addict biker and I didn't like how he treated my friend. I moved out and he moved in. Rochelle and I parted ways for a few years and life just kept rolling along.

I started working for the ambulance service. Rochelle dumped biker dude and got into journalism school, started working for a radio station doing traffic, then the morning show. We both felt like we were transcending our pasts and really making it in the world. Then she got sick and stopped talking to me.

She wouldn't return my calls. I brought her a Raggedy Ann doll, because she'd been Ann and I was Andy one Halloween, but it came back to me, unopened. Before I moved away on my boat adventure, I went to the hospital to see her one last time.

I sat at her bedside, moving my chair closer, taking her hand. We talked about our lives, all the crazy times, the fun we'd had. Her hazel eyes brimmed with tears. "I'm only 29 and I'm going to die. It's not fucking fair."

"I know. I miss you already."

"Fuck, eh?"

"Yeah, fuck."

And that was it.

Rochelle died couple of weeks later on Boxing Day. I'm pretty sure she stopped talking to me because it was just too hard to think of saying goodbye.

We all miss you, funny girl.

My Business,
—— Your Business ——

What is my business and what is your business? Seems like a simple question, but if you think about it, we are often so preoccupied with our own thoughts, opinions and judgements about how everyone else "should" be, that we forget about observing our own behavior.

Byron Katie, in her book Loving What Is, *calls our judgements about other people "being in someone else's business" and, according to her, being in the business of other people is what keeps us all suffering.*

I notice that when I am around someone who talks a lot about other people, especially when it sounds judgmental or mean spirited, I just feel uncomfortable and am not as inclined to tell them my deepest secrets. I also notice that if I'm the one speaking ill of someone, even if I think they "deserve" what I'm saying, I don't feel good either.

Being in my own business (I'll speak for myself here) gives me the opportunity to see how what I think, how I move, how I breathe and how I communicate makes my world. No one else is responsible for me.

What's your contribution? Is that going to get you the world you want?

Insensitive

Mom got a new TV and she asked me if I thought my brother Michael would want the old one. I took it as a challenge to reunite my Mom and brother.

I lived in a tiny shared-bathroom suite in Vancouver's Kitsilano district, before it got so trendy you couldn't afford anything. The apartment was a treasure to me – top floor, heritage house, fire escape for my balcony, even a territorial view of the neighborhood. It so happened that my friend Rochelle found a basement suite across the street, where she lived with her two boys. I felt very lucky to be there.

I had no idea that my brother Michael also lived in a basement suite, just around the corner. I bumped into him one day, walking to the door after getting home from my ambulance shift.

"Oh! What are you doing here?" I asked, a little alarmed.

"I live around the corner," he said. "I guess we're neighbors."

Even after all the years since I'd lived at home with him, I was still rattled by childhood memories of our shared violence and neglect. My stomach kept flipping after I went inside to my place and that night my dreams were about slowly sinking in quicksand, not being able to scream.

When Mom left, Michael was six and because he was that age, with so much cognition already formed, already deeply bonded with his mother, he suffered greatly and would never have the stability to work for a living. Now, with his grief at having lost his mother so early, the sexual abuse from our dad, the bullying from mean kids at school which he took out on me with daily beatings, my brother was for the first time living on his own, right around the corner from me.

They say that life never gives us more than we can handle…

I guess it was my way of trying to make things better, so I attempted to broker a mending and connection between him and Mom, wanting to cauterize the gaping wounds that broke us all apart.

I wanted to find a way for us to feel like a normal family, one that could visit without yelling and crying, where fear didn't hang in the air like a bad smell.

I was desperate to see Mom ease her guilt about leaving and equally desperate for Michael to ease his anger and grief. Their pain had stained my life, too, in ways that I couldn't have even expressed at the time and so I was hoping Mom could give Michael a TV as a gift, which might help fix something. And even though in my guts it didn't feel right, I pressed on, orchestrating their meeting with my sheer will.

It'd been a long time since Mom and Michael were together, about twenty years, give or take. She was gone for nine years of my childhood, but I'd been seeing Mom again since I was twelve, shortly before I left home. Michael, four years older than me, had stayed stuck in the trap he'd grown up in, until my dad had to sell the house and they went their separate ways.

My dad died a couple of years after that, so now I had the chance to be the family savior, finally bringing Mom and Michael together! It would be a reunion and we'd all be a family again.

My first mistake was to not let Michael know we were coming to his place, or to ask permission to come, for that matter. I hadn't even thought of that.

Mom was awkward with people at the best of times and it was doubly difficult for her to see her youngest son again, for the first time in many years, bearing the gift of a used TV set to somehow bridge the chasm between them. I knew the plan was stupid and bound to fail, but I was too ignorant and frantic to know what else to do.

"I don't think he'll want this old thing," she told me. "He might not want to talk to me."

"Mom, stop freaking out about it. He'll love the TV. He watches tons of TV. Hop in a cab and come down there and I'll meet you outside his place. We'll carry it in, then you two can talk and I can just go and leave you guys on your own. It'll be fine."

Mom's taxi pulled up to Michael's place and the two of us struggled the giant tube TV out of the back seat and sideways-walked it down to his door. I knocked and he appeared, stunned, gaping, pale and silent, wordlessly staring at us.

"We brought you a TV. Mom brought you a TV. She thought you'd like it," I said hopefully.

Nothing.

"Um, it's yours. You can have it. Mom wants to be friends with you. Aren't you going to say anything? Can we come in?"

Nothing.

"You could say, 'Thanks, Mom.'"

Nothing.

The door creaked shut leaving us standing there.

When I looked at Mom, it was one of the worst expressions I've ever seen on someone's face. Worse than dread, it was the fulfillment of decades of dread, now right here on her face. The full impact of how insensitive I was to them both was like a fist slamming into my chest.

I'd learned to push away all my pain and ignore red flags and warning signals my whole life, becoming more insensitive to myself and therefore to others, in order to survive. Now, here it was, my clumsy fucking coping mechanisms, hurting the people I so most wanted to spare.

The cab was still there and Mom rushed to it, slamming the door and waving at me as it drove off, one hand covering her face and an ocean of sorrow.

On my way to work the next morning, driving by Michael's house, I saw the TV sitting on the curb with a sign on it.

"Free. Take It Away."

I never told Mom what became of the TV and she never asked.

—— Plants and People ——

As long as I can remember, planting, watering and weeding *has been a solace for me. Pulling weeds feels cathartic and cleansing. You have to pull them by the roots, though, or they just come back stronger and choke out the tender baby plants.*

Over time I've pulled a lot of personal weeds from my life. Bad habits, lies, people who choked out what I wanted to grow...I learned to dig deep to extract the noxious elements. I've found that I have to weed regularly, and then cultivation of something good can keep the weeds from coming back.

In the permaculture way of thinking, weeds are not called "invasive." Plants that grow very quickly in places where they are not cultivated – often smothering food sources, using precious nutrients and water – are known as "opportunistic" plants. They find a place to insert themselves, often in disturbed soil, and then they are hard to get rid of. They keep reproducing.

Just like bad habits.

Like people, plants need the right care to thrive. If you don't put a seed in the ground deep enough, it won't be stable and it won't stand up properly. We all need deep roots to feel secure and able to stand tall. If we don't get the right start, just like a plant we will struggle.

Some compost, the right nourishment, regular water and, most of all, light, and pretty much any plant will grow. But missing any one of those things, plants are stunted and can't yield fruit.

You can't give what you don't have and in that way, too, plants are just like people.

When the weather's hot I try to water the garden every day and sometimes there's a section that doesn't get enough, so it gets dried out and stressed. It's always those plants that are invaded by aphids, sucking the juice out of the stalks, till they keel over and die.

Even the bugs can sense when there is weakness and then they attack. All the other plants that have enough water are fine, but the one who's starting to wilt becomes a victim...

Peter Sellers plays Chance, a simple minded gardener, in the late '70s comedy *Being There*. When his employer dies, the naïve Chance, who has lived his whole life on the estate, is forced to venture into the outside world.

As the film goes on, in response to his encounters with people, Chance the gardener, whose name is misunderstood as "Chancy Gardiner," can only answer with what he knows – basic, practical statements about the garden and weather. Some people dismiss him as an idiot, yet others have great interest in what Chance the gardener says.

Interpreting his lack of worldliness as profound wisdom, the wealthy elite, who are looking for meaning in their shallow lives, proclaim Chance to be a genius, even a potential candidate for president.

No matter what he is asked, Chance is only capable of speaking about his observations from days spent watering, transplanting, weeding and devotedly tending all the plants in his care.

And though he has no idea what they are speaking of, when he is asked about the stock market or politics, Chance's slow and ponderous statements somehow strike a chord causing people to consider how all things in a garden may be applied to life.

The message to me is that seemingly mundane things like plants, birds, wind, rain and sun hold the greatest wisdom. If we take the time to notice, there are all kinds of parallels in how plants and animals live and how we humans live. Nature is always speaking to us. We only need to listen.

Hornby Island

Hornby is a small BC Gulf Island off the coast of Vancouver Island. It's in a kind of "banana belt" of warm tides and winds, so the summers are particularly balmy and mild which attracts a huge influx of yuppies, hippies, hipsters, and "shrubbies," the islanders' name for young twenty something kids who become a nuisance when they squat in the woods on private property.

Mom and me on Hornby Island enjoying the wind

The island is also home to many artists and Americans avoiding the draft who came in the 60's and never left. I lived there for a year in my early twenties and am still not sure which "category" I fit into, but I sure loved that place.

One of my boyfriends had a brother who lived there with his wife, so we came over and found a great place to live right away on Shingle Spit Road. It was a tiny cabin on twenty-five acres with a view to the south and a big open field. The rent was about $200 a month, which we were pretty sure we could scrape together.

Steve's brother was a prawn fisherman and he generously gave us lots of huge frozen prawns to get us off to a good start, which was great, because we had hardly any money.

At our cabin, an old claw foot bathtub sat outside and a spigot shot hot water into it so you could lay there at night soaking while gazing at the stars. There was a wood stove, but we needed wood, so the landlord allowed us to chop down the four giant, dead and dry maple trees out front. We chopped and chopped and ended up with more than enough wood to use and we even sold some and managed to pay another month's rent, as well as buy a few other things.

Life was pretty free and easy there since neither of us was working for a couple of months. We were benefiting from a season of what Canadians call "enjoyment insurance" from tree planting and fruit picking, so we took full advantage of all the island could offer.

We played naked tennis at Tribune Bay Beach and scrambled on the low tide rocks at Whaling Station Bay, gathering fresh oysters for dinner. The firewood money bought us a Honda 80 scooter which, though gutless, was enough to get us both around, when we weren't walking or hitching rides.

Every Friday was pizza night at the Cardboard House Bakery and we'd often call in our order, then fly over there on the scooter wearing gumboots and gray woolen Stanfield undershirts, which are widely considered "de rigueur" for anyone living in the boonies.

Eating the fresh, hot pizza with feta and artichokes while lying in our "poor man's hot tub" outside the cabin next to the woodpile was about as good as it gets on the West Coast. We felt like royalty and life was good.

On Sunday nights we'd go to a privately-owned co-op property where the residents would allow the rest of the island to use their very special sauna. The sauna was a work of art, built entirely of driftwood and in the shape of a giant mushroom, with huge cedar shingles several feet long and wide. Heat came from a very large, handmade cast-iron stove, which looked like a locomotive and glowed red when hot, keeping the sauna at almost unbearable temperatures.

First you'd walk into a "communal change room" where you hung your clothes on a driftwood hook and then slipped into the steaming hot room, where curved logs, cut lengthwise in half, created matching benches to sit on, three tiers deep. It was dark and you couldn't tell who was there, which I always liked. And when you became too hot and couldn't take it anymore, you just got up, dripping with sweat, and slid through the overlapping inner-tube rubber doors, a weird experience in itself, like being born into the cool night.

There you were, naked in the darkness, where all you could see were stars and maybe the moon reflected on the pond, frogs and crickets so loud that they seemed to be the only things existing as you stepped carefully onto a board leading to the water, jumping in to feel the cold, the life. The slimy mud between your toes tickled, as you crawled up the other side on the slippery rock steps. Then you did it all over again.

I only lived there a year, but time went slowly, I made friends, and I think I really healed a lot there, enjoying a safe, comforting retreat time in such a beautiful place. I had a cat named Dillon who'd follow me on walks down to the ocean at night, to the pass between Denman and Hornby Islands. We'd sometimes make a fire on the beach, then sit and listen as the whales swam by, softly spouting and calling to one another.

I'll never forget the peace I felt there.

———— SIMPLICITY ————

Our lives are full, more so in the past ten years or so, because of social media. We want to know what's going on and to be a part of it, but there is a price to pay for where we put our time and attention. It comes back to intention and why it is that we feel we must not miss the latest thing. We want to belong, we want to connect and we ultimately want to make a difference. These things start inside of us, in our hearts. And when we experience trauma, it often changes us because we are laid bare, down to the things that matter most.

Everything changes, even if we don't want it to, and then it's time to stand back and look closely at how traumatic experiences have changed us. It's natural to be altered by trauma, and if we can delicately untangle the difficult parts, without the usual distractions, we can see whatever has become insight, so some or even all of the pain can gradually fall away.

It's interesting to see what it's like to unplug for a week from social media and limit email checking to three times a day for less than 15 minutes each session. See how you feel. Watch something new arise.

Tree Planting

Tree planting is a labor-intensive, piece-by-piece job done by hard-working people who hike up and down hills and gullies, planting one tree at a time, trying to keep ahead of the massive clearcuts decimating our forests every day. It's called silviculture, and I spent three seasons of my youth doing this rigorous, yet peaceful job.

We'd start in early spring before it got too hot on the mountain, though often by May or June when it was sunny and warm at sea level, there'd still be snow and freezing temperatures at five thousand feet. You had to come prepared for blistering sun or snow.

My first contract was in May of 1980, in the mountains outside of Pemberton, BC. My boyfriend David and I were hired by a forestry service contractor and we were told we'd be paid ten cents for every tree we planted.

When we looked shocked at how little this seemed to be for what we were sure would be hard work, the contractor told us, "Yeah, by the end of your first couple of days you'll be planting a thousand trees. That's a hundred bucks a day, eh?" We were keen and eagerly paid the extra fifty dollars for our mattock and planting bags, and then we were on our way.

The ground wasn't too bad. I'd heard horror stories of super-steep slopes and bears everywhere, but we saw neither, and, besides, we were young and strong and by the end of the first couple of days we were each planting a thousand trees or more. A hundred bucks in 1980 was nothing to sneeze at either!

The work was hard, but it felt good and I especially loved planting along the tree line at dusk, drinking in the silence, inhaling the crystal clear air and hearing the wolves howling to one another.

The contract was for three weeks and we slept in tents, eating a rough diet of weird, mostly vegetarian food, like oatmeal with garlic, olive oil and nutritional yeast on top for breakfast, lots of peanut butter and apples for lunch, and usually squash and something cheesy for dinner. There were no showers, so you stuck your bum in the stream every couple of days just so you could stand yourself. I think I wore the same woolen Stanfield undershirt and long johns the whole time.

One Sunday afternoon we were all up there, bent over, planting, when we heard a big boom. We figured it was blasting, but then someone mentioned it was Sunday and they don't blast on Sundays. This was years before the internet and we didn't even have radio reception, so it took till we came down off the mountain, weeks later, for us to find out that the big boom we'd heard was Mount Saint Helens erupting.

The next year I worked on a challenging contract up Knight Inlet on the BC coast. We first had to drive to Port McNeill on the northern end of Vancouver Island. Then a fisherman took us on his boat to the head of the inlet, where a helicopter picked us up and flew us into camp. The pay was twenty five cents a tree and the terrain was like I'd heard of in all those horror stories, almost vertical, it seemed.

No one was going to be planting a thousand trees a day here. But in spite of what we knew would be hard work, this was a spectacular place full of eagles and kingfishers, with all kinds of other birds and beasts. I intended to just soak it all in.

One day I was off planting in a little valley all by myself. There was a stream running along the ridge and thick moss everywhere. I was going slow, savoring the smells and beauty of this magical place, when I looked up across the stream and saw just twenty feet away a huge grizzly bear.

I think it was a female, because of how she looked at me - so soft, so deep, and so full of the mystery and majesty of this place. She just gazed at me and kept slowly walking on her side of the stream, her giant paws pushing through the ferns. I hope she felt my respect and awe of her beauty. I think that's why she felt no threat from me and I felt none from her.

I have a great memory of dragging my friend Rochelle along to plant on one contract near Squamish. I don't know what either of us was thinking because she'd recently had her baby Ryan and was still breastfeeding, but she wanted to go so her mom took care of the baby.

Rochelle's caulk boots were two sizes too big and our tent collapsed in the June snowfall. We went out planting the next day and her breasts leaked milk all over her shirt, making us fall down laughing. I told her she needed to go back home so the contractor drove her back down the mountain the next day. I miss that girl. I even miss tree planting.

I figure I must have planted about two hundred thousand trees in my time. Those were some good memories and that's some good karma, eh?

····· WHAT'S IN THE WAY? ·····

We are preoccupied with what we believe will give us happiness, health, prosperity and peace. Actually, it's all about peace, but we just don't know it. If I am happy, healthy and rich, then, the unconscious thinking goes: "I will have safety and therefore, peace."

Peace is the common denominator to which every thought of the future can be distilled. Funny thing is peace may already be present. Maybe there's just something in the way of our experience of peace.

It sounds lofty and all, but here's an example I run into almost daily. Someone comes to me for acupuncture and I take a thorough history, including all that's brought them to having an imbalance requiring treatment.

I dig deep; deeper, most people say, than other health care practitioners, because it all matters. I want to know what they are doing and not doing with diet, exercise, lifestyle, stress and how they care or don't care for themselves.

During the conversation I make notes and it usually becomes clear how much of what the patient is doing is helping to create the illness and keep them sick. Besides the acupuncture and herbal medicine, most of what I advise is what to stop doing in order to regain health. I tell people to: eat less junk, try to slow down so there's less stress, limit alcohol, stop drugs and smoking, work less, play more, spend less time on the computer and more time enjoying time in nature.

All things done in excess are adaptations to stress that get in the way of our connection to ourselves and to the world.

To see what is in the way of all we want to embody requires what Buddhists call "the backward step" and the insight gained will show us what we do to be in "our own way." The "backward step" happens when we take time to stop, breathe and allow a natural process of nervous-system downregulation, getting a chance to switch from fight-or-flight mode, to a more natural, restful and relaxed way of being, which guides us towards stillness.

Our curiosity and what we notice is its own type of intelligence and it helps us see something that might have been there all along. Maybe peace is there when the dust settles... Then we get to notice what is in its way.

. . . .

Hippie Pirates

We bought an old wooden boat. She was a 1942 tri-cabin trawler, oak-ribbed, cedar-planked, with a gum wood keel from stem-to-stern, capped with iron and powered by a six-cylinder Bedford diesel. My then boyfriend Ross and I scraped together enough to get her for a good price and we felt like baron and baroness, knowing this would be our new home.

That's my boat

Our first winter was a bit rough, even by my standards. We tied up at Coal Harbor Marina near Vancouver's famous Stanley Park. It sounds nice, but the boat leaked like a sieve during those rainy months, so we slept with garbage bags on our legs and buckets all over the floor.

We had the cheapest spot in the marina, close to the ramp, and every undulation of the dock squeaked loudly. And our new neighbors were a group of loud drunks who loved sitting on the park bench at the top of the ramp singing sea shanties and breaking out in the occasional fist fight. I felt exposed and triggered there, and even though I loved the boat, I didn't like where we were tied up.

The boat's name was Andromy, which we were told means "fearless" in Greek, though I've asked Greek people about this word and they just look at me funny. But it was good enough for us and, besides, I needed a little courage myself, because I was burning out from my teen years living on the streets, followed by working ambulance on high overdrive so much of the time.

My skin was covered in psoriasis, I slept fitfully at night and I'd wake each morning in tears of dread for the coming day. It was definitely time to change gears and do something different, so we untied from our moorings and took off up the coast.

For three years it was a free, frugal life, collecting driftwood to burn in the tiny wood stove that took the chill off each night, eating seaweed, jigging for cod and throwing the guts in the crab and prawn traps to get the night's dinner. In the summers we'd swim ashore and pick berries or wild apples. We had no money and it didn't matter. Our orange tabby Sid loved the life, too, a far cry from his back-alley beginnings.

There was a whole subculture of people like us, living on old wooden scows, with uncombed hair, gumboots and woolen sweaters. I called our lot "the hippie pirates of the Pacific."

One of my favorite things about living on a boat was knowing that if we didn't like the place, the weather, the people or the feel of where we'd anchored, we could just pull up and leave. That part was very healing for me. I felt like I always had a way out.

We hardly ever tied up to a dock because that cost money, so instead we'd tie up in a quiet cove, swinging on our anchor, listening to the birds and the slapping of the water, and looking at the dark sky. I learned a lot from those days and I take solace in knowing that should everything go to shit here on land, I can always get an old boat and once again become a Hippie Pirate.

Chickens

They are the most economical, sensible creatures to live with. Chickens take up little space, eat your table and kitchen scraps, create fertilizer for your garden and, of course, they lay eggs. All over the world, ever since chickens were first bred and kept for eggs and meat, people have revered this useful, gentle and amicable bird. Right now we just have three hens. At one time though, I had nearly two hundred laying hens, meat birds, turkeys and geese on our little Quadra Island farm.

It all started modestly enough, with my then husband Ross and me getting six Red Rock pullets. Pullets are the teenagers of the chicken world, not quite ready to start their productive egg-laying life.

A friend gave us his tiny, but homey looking, tool shed, sided with cedar shingles and sporting a driftwood-handled door. I gathered more driftwood logs from the beach to use for posts, all about eight inches in diameter and ten-or-so feet long. The posts got plunked into two-foot deep holes and strung with fishing net, generously given by the native band from the loft where they stored nets for their commercial boats. Next, I nailed the net to lumber and buried it in the ground to deter rodents, so the chickens would be safe and cozy in their new home.

Every day I'd grab a hen and lift her up to see if her "vent" was looking appropriately moist and full, the way my chicken book told me it would when she was ready to lay, and soon we had more eggs than we could eat. I put a little sign at the end of the driveway and every so often someone would knock at our door to see if there were any fresh eggs for sale. My first foray into marketing something the farm had produced was a heady thing. I wanted more chickens.

The livestock auction in Black Creek, a ferry ride and half-hour drive away, was once a month. All manner of critters were there and we'd later "rescue" as many as we could. One of the first critters I bought there was an Angora bunny that no one seemed to want. It was all alone in a cage, fluffy and gray. I got it for fifty cents and was delighted to take bunny home and put it in a large outdoor area I'd used for a dog run. Sadly, the next morning I walked outside just in time to see a wily owl swoop down to grab bunny and fly into a nearby tree, where bunny was eaten. I tried not to cry. You have to be a bit tough to be a farmer.

This day at the auction I was excited to see that the local commercial egg producer was culling all of their one-year-old Rhode

Island Red laying hens. They sat pathetically in cages, as they'd lived for all of their short lives. The cages were eighteen-by-twelve inches and that space housed three birds, thin and almost featherless from pecking one another, and "de-beaked," a grotesque practice of clipping off the end of their beaks to prevent them from drawing blood when they obsessively pecked, bored with nothing else to do. I knew we could give them a better life than this so I was excited to start the bidding.

We ended up with one hundred birds at fifty cents each. The best way to transport them was in paper feed sacks with air holes, so that they would not be further traumatized by the ride home in the pick-up truck.

We made another fenced area of grass, small alders and other bushes, and a coop repurposed from an old shed found on the property would be their new home. One-by-one we carefully cut open the bags and watched the shaky birds walk around for the first time, learning how to peck at dirt and bugs, dust bathing, eating grass and beginning a new life, more as was intended for one of God's creatures.

Miraculously, in a few weeks, not only did their feathers start to come back in, but their clipped beaks even regrew, shiny and straight. True to their breed, those hens were hard-working layers, each producing at peak all year long and they were so docile and "friendly" that they'd crouch down and let me pick them up for a "chicken cuddle" any old time. Maybe they kind of knew that I'd saved them. I find that "rescue" animals are like that. They never forget that you cared.

The next month we went back to the auction and bought another bunch of hens to add to the flock and by this time my egg production was such that we were selling wholesale to the local store. I respected them, loved them even, and I always felt grateful for how much pleasure and peace of mind those birds gave me.

Sheep

We started with six sheep and got many more over time. The first ones were six-month-old purebred Romney ewes. Ross and I got them from a lady who raised Romneys and herding dogs. We got to choose the ewes right off the field, already bred by her ram, so that in five months we'd have lambs!

Then, after a couple of months, we went to the auction and got several more, for an eventual flock of close to fifty ewes and lambs. I was so excited. The whole thought of sheep sounds bucolic, which it is, and easy, which it isn't. I love hearing people say, "We could just put a couple of sheep on the pasture and raise some lambs." There's more to it, though. A lot more.

We fenced six pastures in order to rotate them, so when they grazed the grass down low, they were shifted to new pasture to avoid getting worms from exposure to their own abundant feces. That part's actually fun and easy. You open the gate, the sheep all bah their heads off and go running into the fresh green grass they've been eyeing all week. They also need fresh water and hay daily, and grain, too, as they get closer to lambing, to ensure big strong babies.

Then there is the shearing, which I stubbornly wanted to learn to do myself, so I rode around with the local shearer and learned the trade, eventually getting my own electric clipper set-up. And yes, I sheared them, carded and spun my own wool, and knitted giant, thick things that could stand up all on their own. I never was very good at it at all, but I enjoyed hosting half-a-dozen women every week at the house for our spinning guild. Everyone brought their own wheels and fiber and we'd drink tea or, sometimes, a lot of wine.

When they start getting close to their time, it's good to check the ewes' rear ends often to see if they are "poufy" and pink, then you need to set aside an area for baby lamb to come into the world. Often lambs were born at night and if it was cold we'd set up a heat lamp in the barn in the lambing area. You also have to be prepared to reach inside a ewe and help her if the lamb is coming out the wrong way or if she is having twins or triplets. Most times it all turned out fine. Of course there was the occasional sad and tragic lamb death, but that was seldom.

When the lambs are about one hundred pounds and around six-months old, you have to decide who to keep and who to take to the abattoir for butchering. If you want to expand your flock, you keep the biggest ewe lambs, from sets of twins or triplets, from mothers who lamb easily and milk well. Keeping lambs from twin or triplet litters increases your chances of getting higher yields from the flock as those young ones become productive ewes. And unless you need another ram or want to sell one, the ram lambs are your meat for the winter.

Feeding time for the lambs

I liked our abattoir. He was a big man, gentle and kind, who always admired the sheep we brought him. "Those look like a good, healthy bunch. It's been a nice spring with lots of pasture, eh? Okay. Thanks and let them know at the counter how you want the meat done up."

I always felt pretty good leaving there, knowing the animals would be treated humanely and wouldn't be scared. Ironic as it may sound, it was good to know that the person killing them cared.

In week or so they'd call for us to pick up the boxes of meat, all labeled as per each customer's order. And they gave me the pelts, too. Into the back of the pickup would go plastic garbage bags filled with pelts, all ready for me to start tanning. That, too, was a lot of work and like any good farmer, I didn't like to see things go to waste, so I'd tan all the pelts (a hugely stinky, disgusting and labor-intensive process) then sell them to our customers.

The sheep are a great memory. I love all animals and have an especially soft spot for cloven-hoofed beasts like sheep, goats, deer and llamas. They are peaceful, gentle creatures and I feel lucky to have raised them.

☯

· · · · · KIDNEY TIME · · · · ·

Adrenal glands sit atop our kidneys, which are encased in their own special sacs, outside the abdominal cavity and partially protected by the posterior ribs. These tiny dark pyramids are the workhorses of the endocrine glands, including ovaries, thyroid, gonads, pancreas, thymus and pineal glands, giving everyone the signal to start producing chemicals to make the whole system work.

Most of us have heard of "adrenal burn out," what happens when adrenals have been overworked by chronic stress, to the point of producing too much for too long. Cortisol, an important anti-inflammatory chemical, is overproduced and the blood vessels and immune system break down. When this happens we feel terrible and we get sick, which brings me back to the kidneys:

Caring for kidneys (and therefore the adrenal glands) as per the uncanny ancient wisdom of the East, can be as simple as starting to watch what time of day we take for some rest. In traditional Five-Elements theory of Chinese medicine, all the organs and meridians have special times of day to nurture them and the hours between five and seven pm are the best time to rest and rejuvenate our kidneys.

The five to seven pm rush hour is not our society's usual time to be putting our feet up, but we can try. Even sitting down for a few conscious breaths, closing our eyes and drinking a cool glass of water, allows our adrenals to take a break and the whole nervous system to change gears to regenerate all the endocrine glands. See if you can imagine "breathing" a black or dark-blue color "into your kidneys." Exhale stress. Try it. You'll like it.

Grand Forks

I left the farm on Quadra Island with a couple of garbage bags full of clothes and six of my favorite sheep in the pickup. I think I would have turned right around if he'd ever just said, "Don't go." I was waiting for that, but the words never came. And I said goodbye to my dog. I told her I'd be back. Her eyes said, "Don't go," but I went anyhow.

Driving in the August heat with such a load and feeling the craziness of what I was doing, my mouth was dry and my heart pounded. There was so much weight from the thousand or so pounds of sheep in the back of the half-ton truck that the front wheels lifted up and sort of hovered over the road, especially when I went uphill, making steering pretty sketchy.

I was heading for Grand Forks, for no good reason, except that a girl I knew lived there and I'd been out once to visit her. She had horses and a big house and said I could visit any time. So here I was, coming there with my sheep.

It was a perilous drive through the mountain passes, with the sheep panting in the back, wondering where I was taking them. I stopped in Princeton to get something to drink and they sucked water from bottles I held to their mouths. One of them, Lizzy, my favorite ewe, eyed me suspiciously.

Two ferries and six hours or so later, I arrived in Grand Forks, BC, pulling into a gas station to fill up and use the pay phone to call

Tammy and let her know I'd arrived. The girl at the gas station asked me where I was from. "I drove from Quadra Island and I'm going to stay a while."

"Yeah, Grand Forks is a good place to hide out," she said, without looking up as she took my twenty bucks.

Tammy looked less than thrilled when I pulled up and let the anxious sheep out on her lawn to graze. "What are you going to do with them?" she asked.

"Oh, I'm not sure. I'm hoping to find a farm to rent or something." But I really hadn't even thought it through. I felt stupid, scared and had no idea what I was going to do with myself or the sheep. I'd left my farm, my dog and my marriage with Ross, without really knowing why, but just running, feeling the familiar shock of flinging myself, out of control, into the unknown.

She was kind, though, and told me I could stay until I found something else, so I began to relax for a few days. Then one evening a man in a big fancy pickup rolled up the driveway.

"Hi there," he said, friendly and waving as he stepped out of the truck. "Do you ladies know anyone who'd like to care-take our ranch down on the river? We have a couple of horses, two dogs and two cats and we'll be gone for the winter so we need someone to live there and watch things for us."

"I will! I have some sheep but I can make sure they stay out of trouble there," I almost shouted.

"Well that sounds great! We have lots of hay for your sheep and a big barn that they can be in at night. It's two hundred and fifty acres and there's a nice guest place, too. Come on down and meet my wife Maureen. I'm Burt. Nice to meet you!"

So, just like that, less than a week after getting there, I had a place for both me and my sheep in Grand Forks. It was true serendipity at work.

Burt and Maureen seemed to be nice people. Clearly they had a lot of money and everything was picture perfect, as if Martha Stewart had been there and waved her magic wand. My little place was a one bedroom suite attached to the large garage and shop. It had a woodstove, kitchen and bathroom, and was furnished, too. I was delighted.

The sheep were in heaven, no longer regarding me as crazy, since they had tons of hay to eat, acres of pasture to run on, and the ewes were fattening up quickly, having been bred just before I left my farm back on Quadra. Lizzy was now looking at me like I was a genius. I felt like one, too. Everything was going just great.

I badly missed my farm, my dog, my friends, my life, but I didn't know how to change directions now. I only knew how to push through my sadness and discomfort and carry on. I was good at that, but not so good at making wise decisions and I was soon to learn another lesson about ignoring my instincts.

The ranch owners were going to Hawaii for the winter but the day before they left, a big truck arrived with twelve Standardbred brood mares that I'd have to care for. They were beautiful alright, all running and kicking and farting like horses do, happy to be free to run wild in the endless fields.

But Burt hadn't told me I'd be caring for them, too, besides the other horses, dogs and cats, not to mention my sheep, but I didn't say anything. I didn't want to make any waves and lose my place there. I was kind of scared, but I pushed the feelings down deep.

They left in their fancy truck, waving goodbye to me, smiling like everything was fine. I waved, too, smiling and feeling dread rising in my throat like stone.

The weather had been warm and sunny since I'd arrived there, but November came much too soon, then it started to snow.

1996 was a bad snow year for a lot of places and in Grand Forks it piled in drifts so fast that the downed tree Burt left me for firewood was buried in a couple feet of snow. He told me I could "Just get someone to buck it up and then chop it and put it in the shed." One of Tammy's neighbors had a chainsaw and, sure, he'd buck it for me, if I spent the day plucking chickens outside with his wife as the snow came down. As each bird was decapitated, it was handed to me to scald in a pot of hot water and then pull out the feathers. My hands were freezing and I didn't feel like a genius anymore.

I just couldn't get warm. The baseboard heaters in my little suite didn't seem to work at all and I'd been chopping wood like a maniac, stoking the fire every couple of hours, trying to keep it going because the water pipes were starting to freeze. Then the power went out and the coils in the water troughs couldn't keep them from freezing and the horses all got influenza, running around wild-eyed with runny noses, coughing.

I called the vet and he came out with a giant-sized bottle of penicillin and syringes, telling me to give them a shot twice a day. There were fourteen horses altogether and I didn't know how to get them to go where I wanted them. Wielding the lunge whip that hung in the shed, I flailed around the fields, chasing the horses in two feet of snow, with a giant needle to jab in their necks.

It didn't work very well but a kind neighbor saw me one day and showed me how to lure them with a bucket of grain, which worked like a charm.

Meanwhile, my sheep were starting to lamb and the barn was pretty far from my place, so I made a trail in the snow to trudge through several times a night, in order to check them and make sure they were lambing out okay, while carrying a rifle for the cougars that I was told were around and could smell the blood.

Most of them delivered their lambs without help but one extra cold night I must have slept through and not gotten up to check on them. I was pretty sure one of the one of the ewes would be having triplets, so I wanted to be sure that they were coming out alright, but when I got there I found that it was so cold when they were born that two of them just froze to the barn floor and died. Devastated, I laid there on the frozen boards with them, wishing I could just disappear, as the mama ewe tried to lick them back to life.

And the snow kept coming. I was freezing and had little food. Tammy was busy with a new guy in her life and I figured she really didn't want me around, so I stopped calling her.

Burt called from Hawaii and I told him how cold it was and he said, "Oh yeah, well I turned off the baseboards because you had lots of wood and I didn't want to give you carte blanche while we were away."

Carte blanche. I was stunned. Carte blanche, like I was lying around in a bikini with a margarita in my hand. I hung up the phone, trying to figure out what to do next. I had to get out of there.

Meanwhile, the horses had to be fed. I rumbled through the snow, driving a tractor with chains on the tires and a spike on the forks so it could pick up the huge round bales of hay I brought to the horses. Once the bales were dropped, I had to jump off the tractor and cut the string, which held each bale together. But because the bales had been sitting outside uncovered, the string I had to cut was under two feet of frozen snow, and having no luck with my pocket knife, I had to chop through it with an axe, which wasn't easy in the frigid temperatures.

Then the horses ran away.

The cattle guard at the entrance filled up with several feet of hard-packed snow so the horses were able to escape and ran up the road, with me chasing them in the tractor, until another rancher saw them running and helped me herd the escaped mares back in. Together, we put up some wire for a temporary fence so they couldn't get out again.

Another disaster to chalk up.

Then, one day when I was at my wit's end, the local farrier came by to work on the horses' feet. He knew the place well, having come there before to work, and Burt had asked him to look in on things while they were away and trim some of the horses' hooves.

I was in the barn trimming my ewes feet when he arrived. "How have things been going out here for you? Are you all on your own? Nice sheep you've got there. I have some sheep, too. My name's Paul."

"Hi," was all I could get out before bursting into tears and blubbering out the whole saga of the past few months on the ranch, trying to get along in the snow. "All the fucking horses got sick and my fucking lambs froze and I have no heat in that place where I stay and I'm freezing," I sobbed.

All he said was, "You can put your sheep in my pickup and come to my farm if you want." It was music to my ears and I didn't need convincing.

Paul's daughter Nicola was just twelve and he was raising her on his own after his divorce. Their ranch had sheep, and lots of horses. I felt welcome and I stayed there more than a year, custom haying in the summer, moving irrigation pipes with Nicola, swimming in the river, watching movies, riding horses, playing with dogs and just feeling loved. It was a strange time in my life, but I'll never forget how it felt to be welcome and have a place to be.

Paul and I drove out every day to tend to the horses and other animals up the valley until the ranch owners got back. I owed the critters that much, but I never spoke to those people again.

Many years have gone by and Paul married a nice woman who loves to be on the farm with him. Nicola has become like the daughter I never had. We connect by email, Skype and Facebook, laughing at memories of all the wacky farm adventures we had, like the time a cougar showed up and started killing sheep, then just lay on the front porch so we couldn't leave the house. We finally had to call the ranger, who had to shoot it, which was sad, but necessary I guess.

Then there was the time one of my lambs was born on a frigid, below-zero night and her ears froze off. She went on to grow into a strong little ewe, but without any ears, looking more like a seal than a sheep, which made Nicola and me laugh every time we saw her.

One of the cows who patrolled the fence line had huge horns and it scared me to walk past her, but Nicola was fearless. "Here cow," she'd say sweetly, when we had to go in the pasture to leave some hay. "Be nice to Rebekah, okay?"

There's so much more to remember, always so much more to say, and it was true: Grand Forks was a great place to hide out for a while.

Things We Think Are Precious

I woke up this morning with the words from Steely Dan's "Reelin' In the Years" in my head. I was thinking about what is precious to me and how that has changed, and also stayed the same, throughout my life.

Mom had a gold ring with a carnelian stone in it and I coveted it for years. Whenever Mom wore it, I'd ask if I could try it on and she'd reluctantly let me, but then grab it back quickly, like I was going to steal it. The ring was given to her when she visited Sweden with her boyfriend Sven, and his father, who liked Mom, gave it to her.

Sven was a kind man and he had been good to Mom after she left her marriage to my dad and lost her kids. She spoke of Sven often, telling me about their adventures in Canada's Arctic, camping in the wilderness where Sven was a geologist and Mom was the cook for his crew. They were going to be married but Sven died suddenly just two years after they met.

The ring was precious to Mom, or even more accurately, it was the memories the ring represented which were precious.

Maybe that was part of the allure for me, not the ring itself but the curious notion that Mom's elusive heart was somehow attached to it. I wanted to feel part of something precious to her. I thought that if she gave this thing to me, I would know I was important to her.

I too had made the ring into something precious.

My older sister, Nora, came up from California to visit Mom whenever she could. I'd had conversations with Nora about "the precious ring," voicing my resentment and disdain that Mom's ring was "more important" to her than I was. Because of my hurt and feelings of abandonment I constantly had about Mom, it seemed like I was in a weird competition with the precious ring for her love.

One weekend I went to Vancouver to see Nora and Mom. I'd just taken off my coat and sat down when Mom said, "Close your eyes and hold out your hand." I did as I was told, thinking she was going to give me a piece of the banana bread I smelled when I came in.

Then I felt the ring slip onto my finger. I kept my eyes closed, not wanting to be disappointed, but I knew the feel of it, the weight of it. With my eyes still shut, I touched the smooth stone and thin band of gold, savoring, trying to take it in.

When I opened my eyes, Mom said, "You deserve this. I want you to have it. I don't need it, but you do."

I'm pretty sure it was hard for Mom to give away her precious ring and I'm also sure that Nora helped her let it go, wanting me to know that I really was important to Mom, more than the ring.

It was a sacrifice for Mom to give the ring to me and that mattered.

I wore it often on the ring finger of my left hand, showing her, "Look Mom, I wear your ring on my marriage finger because I love you and this ring is so special." I wanted her to know that I honored the little piece of her heart she'd given me with that ring.

It's not the ring that's precious, but the memory it represents. Every time I feel scared or nervous, like when I have to present a talk or workshop, or any other time fear, insecurity and self-doubt creeps in, I wear the ring to remind me that loving and being loved are our most precious gifts.

JOY AND
—— CELEBRATION ——

You hear a lot about how it's important to let out painful emotions like sadness, grief and anger. Keeping these emotions inside binds them to us and without air and light, they fester. There are people who have made it a habit to hurt others with words, actions and beliefs and in doing this, they have failed to move beyond their own pain. Striking out at others is perhaps a knee-jerk, maladaptive attempt to demonstrate how pain feels, to engender empathy in the other, but it never works to heal anything.

On the other hand, expressing joy and celebration is just as important as processing and releasing pain. I've been someone who's had to re-learn how to let my heart open to joy and to celebrate with happiness when something stirs my soul to smile. I've learned that not letting out my joy also hurts, and it doesn't just hurt me.

No matter how we try, we can't selectively numb pain without also numbing joy and that's a good thing.

Her Church

Mom was what you'd call a "lapsed Catholic." Even though it's how she grew up, sent to a convent school as a young girl and made to pray the holy rosary daily, she was never the pious type. Her church was the beach.

Mom at her beloved English Bay Bathhouse

I must have been three years old, just before Mom left; I have a faint memory of Mom, Dad, Michael and me, all piled in the car to go to Cultus Lake with my Aunt Hazel and Uncle George. Mom and Hazel were good friends, so I think she and George came along as "buffers" to keep the fights between my parents to a dull roar.

We stayed in a cabin at the edge of the lake. Mom and Hazel got up early in the mornings to swim and took me along with them. Even though I consciously don't remember it, there's still a visceral memory of Mom's hands around my waist, swooshing me back and forth at the lakeshore. "Paddle baby! Weeee!"

Our joy in the water together became a touchstone for us.

After she was on her own for a few years, Mom moved to Vancouver's "Wild West End" off Davie Street, just a few blocks from English Bay. In those days, Mom was at the height of her wildness, too: divorced, no kids and lots of boyfriends, going out dancing at night, and not much time for me. But if I ever wanted to find her on a hot summer day, I knew where she'd be.

She was one of the very few who had her own locker at English Bay, next to the changing rooms, where she kept a spare towel, bathing suit, cap and Bain du Soleil suntan lotion, to ensure she had the best tan of all her sun-lizard friends at the beach.

Mom was on a first-name basis with the lifeguards, too, and I cringed, watching her shameless teenage flirting with them all.

"Oh, hello Brian! If I get into trouble out on the water I sure hope it's you who comes to save me! Tee hee hee."

I'd show up whenever I could, always unannounced, finding her sitting up against the wall of the bathhouse, face tilted upward to heaven, slathered in oil, looking blissful, at peace, like there was nowhere on earth she'd rather be. She was in her church.

It both fascinated and repulsed me, how she could so blithely sun herself, while I held so much resentment and rage at her for not being the mother I needed her to be. She looked like she hadn't a care in the world, while I struggled with no place to call home.

"Hi Mom."

"Oh! My beautiful daughter! Brian, this is my daughter Rebekah."

"Really Mary? You don't look old enough to have a daughter!"

"Oh Brian…tee hee hee."

Barf. "I'll go change into my suit."

The sand was burning hot and it was a long way from the bathhouse to the water. Walking past the beach logs, all the risqué bathing attire, the smell of coconut oil like a thick fog, we held hands.

It was always Mom who reached for my hand first. She'd grab it and squeeze tightly, looking straight ahead. I think it was easier for her to not look at me. It might have broken the sacred spell.

"The water's warm today, but a little choppy because of the wind. Let's swim way out there to the slide. I'm a good swimmer so I'll keep an eye on you. Come on Rebekah, let's go!"

Mom was indeed a good swimmer and I'd follow her steady crawl, watching her look back over her shoulder for me every few strokes. We'd usually stay in for an hour or more, until we both could hardly move our arms.

"Here, take my hand so we can both walk faster over the hot sand," she'd say, looking straight ahead again.

Once we got back, she'd usually send me for fish and chips at the beach stand. "With lots of salt and pepper, eh!" she'd call out.

Eating silently together, smiling at nothing, I'd compare the shape and color of our legs side-by-side, utterly happy and content for no reason at all.

····· YOU AND YOUR LIVER ·····

Ancient concepts of other cultures are blended into our language and thinking. For instance, in the Five-Element theory of traditional Chinese medicine (tcm), the liver meridian is associated with the color green and the emotion of anger. In Western society, the color green can be associated with envy and anger. Think of being green with envy or the image of The Incredible Hulk.

In my first few months of Chinese medicine school, I patiently sat in the classroom, learning about the Five Elements, though honestly it all seemed like gibberish to me. Coming from a Western background of emergency medicine, I was skeptical of what seemed like pure philosophy rather than scientifically-based theories and I had to bite my tongue as I listened to lectures about the acupuncture points and Chinese herbs.

Though, as I began to see that traditional Chinese medicine's view of the mind and emotional connection with health and illness had a lot in common with some of the modern Western concepts of mind and body synergy, I became very interested. I'd been reading a lot about the science of psychoneuroimmunology, which is the study of the psyche, emotions and immune system and how those things all work together.

Emotions are intimately linked to physical symptoms in both Chinese medicine and the modern science of psycho-neuroimmunology. When anger is repressed, it turns into depression and hurts us and when we overindulge our anger, we can hurt ourselves and others, too. Then body, mind and spirit all become out of balance and we can get sick.

Interestingly, the syndrome of repressed emotion in Chinese medicine is known as "liver qi stagnation." So, in order to smooth out the liver qi, traditional Chinese medicine uses diet, meditation, right breathing and the practice of martial arts like qigong.

Taoism, the root of Chinese medicine, is the timeless study of nature's influence on everything, including humans, as part of nature. It encourages us to be like bamboo, bending and not breaking, while working to become more flexible and less rigid in our thinking and opinions.

What it comes down to for me is awareness of how I am thinking, speaking and behaving, and then trying to be fluid, to "be like water," as martial arts master Bruce Lee would say. Good advice and something to aspire to.

. . . .

Not Your Family

I'd always been curious about my Mom's side of the family, but I never knew them. Because Mom left when I was three, I hadn't been able to meet her twelve siblings from their big Catholic clan. Her father had been a famous physician and surgeon, her mother a society lady who painted still lifes of fruit and portraits of kittens.

The children had nannies to care for them and they all lived in a big mansion in Summerside, Prince Edward Island. It all seemed like a fairytale to me.

Mom had been somewhat estranged from most of her family for many years, since she'd married my father against her own father's wishes. She fell in love with the poor, uneducated but handsome man from the Canadian Airforce, whom she'd met when he was twenty and she was just nineteen, while he was on duty in Labrador. They ran away together, all the way to Vancouver, BC, where they spent their married life and had four children.

When I was twelve, I reconnected with my Mom. We'd meet downtown, or often at the beach, where Mom liked to spend a lot of time sunning, swimming and hanging out with all her other tanned friends, wrinkled, brown and glistening with suntan oil.

During our visits she'd often refer to her parents or brothers and sisters and the times she spent on the beautiful beaches of Prince Edward Island, where she grew up. When she spoke of how it was "back home" I'd feel all anxious and my heart would race, like I was running. But if I asked any questions about seeing those people, my family, Mom would go quiet and say, "They are not your family. They are my family." And the subject was closed.

I didn't understand. Weren't her relatives, my relatives? Why was Mom so proprietary about them and why didn't she want to share them with me or me with them?

It was always a sore spot for us both and even decades later Mom would casually mention that she had just come back from PEI and had a wonderful time with "her family," which of course just twisted me up inside. Sometimes one of her brothers or sisters came to Vancouver to visit and she'd tell me about it after they'd left.

Years went by like this and resentment built for me, fueling my low self-esteem and belief that my mother didn't care and never would. I believed she was ashamed of me and that was why she didn't want me to be around "her family."

I called her one evening. She told me she was booking a flight to PEI to visit with "her family" and I felt a lump rise in my throat, as I started to say what I'd never said before to her.

"But Mom, why don't you ever take me with you? Why have you all these years kept your family from being my family? It really hurts me."

The phone went dead as she hung up on me. I sobbed and threw it across the room. In a few minutes it rang again.

"I booked a flight to PEI next week," Mom said slowly.

"I know. You told me. Why are you telling me this again?"

"Because," Mom said. "Because I'm not going without you. I booked your flight, too, so I hope you can take the time to meet our family."

I don't know quite what it was that changed Mom's mind and heart, but I am forever grateful because we did go together to PEI and it was amazing. We swam in that warm Atlantic Ocean and lay on that red sand and I met our family, who all loved me and treated me like one of them, because I am one of them. Always was, always will be.

—— IS IT TRUE ——

We have thoughts, beliefs and belief systems based on our experience and influences in life. We live our lives based on what we believe to be true about ourselves, friends, family, strangers and other groups or people we have labeled and put into categories. We believe what we think is true, because we're accustomed to thinking and believing it is. What we think becomes the truth in our minds. Or does it?

Questioning our beliefs can be powerful stuff if we are willing. I was teaching a secondary-trauma workshop today for a social service agency and one person was brave enough to do this exercise with me in front of his peers. I asked him to voice a judgement or belief he had, then to ask these four questions from what spiritual teacher Byron Katie calls The Work: Is it true? Are you absolutely sure it's true? How do you feel, behave, treat others when you believe that thought? Who would you be without that thought?

He was thoughtful, took his time and expressed his long-held belief to the group. We went through the four questions together, slowly allowing him to look closely at what he'd held for so long.

He was genuinely curious, gentle and, above all, carefully asking the questions, wanting to see what he would find. He wasn't being asked to drop anything or to change anything, just to look and notice – a powerful thing we seldom take time to do, when it comes to our own thoughts.

We may have good reasons for the beliefs we hold. We use our beliefs to protect us and they can be good survival mechanisms for a while. But at some point we might find that old beliefs and ways of being don't fit anymore. Something's changed and we just can't feel the same way we did. Maybe once we look closer and ask four questions, the old ideas drop, without us even trying to drop anything.

Or maybe not, or not right now…

Try asking yourself, when you have your next judgmental thought: "Is it true?" Hmmm…

Alcatraz

They were kept separate from society, banished to an island, where they would pay for their crimes. Humans instinctively know that the worst kind of punishment is isolation, because it dehumanizes both the captive and the captors. At Alcatraz, you were not supposed to feel human. You'd lost that right.

In 1989, Mom and I made a rare trip together to visit my sister Nora in the San Francisco Bay area. I was working for the ambulance service and also in college, studying sciences, thinking of becoming a chiropractor.

Travelling with my Mom to see my sister seemed like such a "normal" thing for us to do together and now we were all going on a little excursion. For an outing on our first day there, Nora suggested a "nice boat trip," which Mom was excited about. Mom loved boat rides. It'd be grand.

With the sun shining and wind blowing in our hair, our boat approached the island.

Alcatraz loomed, ominous and menacing, just like in the movies. My guts churned, my neck prickled and I tried to stuff down a strange and growing dread by crunching on a couple of Chicklets from my purse.

Like watching apes behind bars in a zoo, this whole thing felt wrong and I didn't know how to express what I felt, so I tried to pretend I felt something else. It wasn't that hard to do. I was used to ignoring what my guts told me...

As we filed off the boat, we were blasted by a carnival-like loudspeaker voice carping: "Welcome to Alcatraz! You're visiting one of the world's most famous prisons, where criminals like Al Capone and the Bird Man of Alcatraz did hard time."

Mom and me at Alcatraz

I watched the color drain from Mom's face as she screamed at Nora and me, "What kind of place did you bring me to? I want to get out of here right now. Are you out of your minds? I'm getting back on that boat."

I could feel Mom's horror and without even realizing it, something like horror also swirled in me, seeing what was slowly unfolding. Mom was having a fit, yelling at us in front of the startled passengers, moving down the boat ramp, while I just tried to numb out and pretend I didn't feel anything. After all, she'd looked so happy on the way across. We were all doing so well, being a normal family, on a nice outing. Why did she always have to fuck things up when all the attention wasn't on her?

"Come on Mom," I sniped. "You don't always have to be Mary, Mary, quite contrary. You can't go back right now. We're here for a couple of hours, so just come inside and go on the tour with us. It'll be interesting."

"I'll wait outside. You go. I'm not going in there." Mom sulked into a sunny spot on the rocky shore, perched tensely on her jacket and looking like she wanted to disappear.

My brother David working in prison laundry

I remember feeling nauseated nd looking back over my houlder as I walked in to Alcatraz, seeing Mom sitting alone, isolated and sulking. I pushed down the urge to run back to her, hold her and tell her how sorry I was that she was hurt.

Instead, I put on a set of headphones and walked along the eerie walls and barred cages, stopping in front of Al Capone's cell.

I'd been standing there a while, when out of the corner of my eye I saw Mom in her yellow jacket. She'd moved in slowly then she stood close to me, silently gripping my arm and staring straight ahead.

Without a word, just her presence and gestures made me understand why we should never have come there. I had not wanted to be in touch with what tore at me, but now, looking at Mom's face, so empty with grief, I would have given anything for us both to be somewhere else.

We left on the next boat and never spoke about it again.

To some people, Alcatraz is an interesting place to visit, but to Mom, the only thing she could see was all the years her oldest son David spent behind bars.

Sorry Mom. I'm so very sorry.

—— KINDNESS ——

Kindness isn't a gesture. We can give objects, money or our time, but when we are moved by the genuine impulse of caring and kindness, it's different and we feel something in us stir. Kindness is far-reaching and it impacts many people, even when we think we are just directing it to one person in one circumstance. We should never underestimate the effects of how we treat one another.

We can show kindness by what we don't do, too. When we choose not to raise our voice when we feel angry, the pause gives a chance for something else. Or when we stop arguing and instead allow another point of view, we get to let down defenses and see what that's like. Becoming less rigid with our long-held opinions is a sign that we are becoming more kind, and that changes everything.

Who are All These Dead People?

I was still working for the ambulance service and had finished my counseling degree and clinical internship, specializing in post-traumatic and critical-incident stress. I was also still teaching the paramedic program, too, and feeling pretty burned out. I took a Reiki course and I liked that and I wasn't sure what I'd do next, but it felt like something new was going to guide me. Then I got invited to a Healing Circle.

I was told it was a First Nations elder named Dwayne who would be sitting with us, but that was all I knew. Everyone was told to bring a gift, so I brought a small bouquet of fresh lilacs from my yard and $20 in an envelope. Tobacco was supposed to be good to bring, too, so I bought a pack of Drum for him.

Dwayne, was a big, middle-aged-looking Native man, with long, straight, black hair in a ponytail. He stared right into my eyes as I walked in, but then he seemed alarmed when I handed him the flowers and my other gifts. I felt a little self-conscious that I'd already done something wrong so I quickly sat on a cushion in the circle, not having a clue what would happen.

He spoke for a few minutes, in a slow, deliberate way, about the traditions of his people and said he was going to "clean" us with the large eagle feather he held in his hand. One-by-one people came to sit in front of him and he'd sometimes ask a question or two, and sometimes nothing at all, then he'd pass the eagle feather in front and behind the person.

Sometimes he'd light some sage or sweetgrass in an abalone shell, then use the feather to wave the smoke all around whoever sat with him. Often the person would cry or laugh and he'd say something like, "Are you feeling better now?"

"Yes," they'd say, or maybe just nod.

"I bet you do," he'd smile. Then they'd go sit down and the next one would get up for their turn.

It didn't look so bad to me and I started feeling comfortable, waiting for when I'd have to sit on the cushion, too. When I sat down, Dwayne was on my right side, just looking at me. He closed his eyes, then passed his hands over my head and down my back.

He didn't say anything and I was starting to get nervous. A few more minutes went by and I just closed my eyes and tried to be very still, while he took deep breaths, coughed, talked to himself and made some weird clicking sounds.

Then he said, "Who are all these dead people standing around you?" My skin instantly felt prickly and freezing cold. I looked at him, but I couldn't speak.

"What do you do for a living?" He asked.

"I'm a paramedic."

"Oooh, I see. When people die, you don't let them go. They are dying and you grab them and say, 'Don't go!' They are all waiting here. I can see them. You are carrying them everywhere with you. Is your back sore?"

"Yes, my back is killing me."

"I'm going to help you. Breathe."

I don't know how long I sat there, but I felt something happening, something releasing in my spine. I cried and cried, sobbing with snot and tears pouring down my face, while Dwayne sang softly, something beautiful like a lullaby. Sweetgrass was fanned all over me with the eagle feather – in my face, down the back of my shirt, under my arms, on the soles of my feet. When I opened my eyes, the circle had closed in and everyone in the room had moved nearer to me. And the back pain I'd had for years was gone.

I had the honor to be invited by Dwayne, with several others, to do a vision quest at his birthplace, which is a time I will never forget. A group of us drove there together with Dwayne, stopping along the way to visit people he knew, bathe in streams, pick nettles and other wild plants, and listen to his stories.

I asked Dwayne while we drove, "Why did you look at me so funny when I first came to the circle?"

"You made me nervous. Because I was allergic to flowers and there you were with a bouquet for me. But my nose didn't run and I was okay, even with those flowers right there. So I thought that was funny and that you were funny, too."

"Oh," I said. "Yeah, that's funny."

Life is full of funny things.

What We Are Good At

When I initially discovered first aid, then ambulance work and teaching, it was a natural fit for me. I'd learned in my crazy, stressful childhood to be quick on my feet and to run on adrenalin, so speeding around in a moving vehicle on the wrong side of the road and patching up broken bodies was right up my alley. I was comfortable (for a while) and the chaos was familiar to me. I was good at it.

In addition to working "on car" for BC Ambulance, I taught a paramedic program for over twenty years at Saint John Ambulance. The training consisted of ten seven-hour days of intense study of anatomy, pathology and trauma, with hours of homework each night. Then in the classroom there were endless practical scenarios on emergency procedures.

At the end of the training there was a rigorous five-hour board exam, which if the students failed, some of them could lose their jobs. I did my best to make it as light and fun as I could for them, but it was pretty heavy stuff and the gravity of pass-or-fail made for an often amped-up bunch of students. Whether I was teaching or in the ambulance, my nervous system was habitually in overdrive; even off the job, I still felt on edge.

During my paramedic work, every time I heard my call sign on the ambulance radio or when I was at the station and the hotline rang, my fight or flight mechanism kicked in. Even though I wasn't literally in danger, my heart would start pounding, then my mouth would go dry and sweat ran down my sides, as my body got ready to spring into action. The uncertainty of what I might face on a call was what triggered me. I'd been hypervigilant all my life, waiting for the next threat and here it was again in another form.

When I'd finish an ambulance shift, the sound of the "hotline" phone ringing a call from dispatch would still echo in my ears and many days I'd drive home crying, with the radio cranked as loud as it could go.

Even once I was safely home, showered and eating dinner, if the telephone rang, my whole system would rev up to save the day once more, in an unconscious, Pavlovian response. My heart raced, sweat ran down my sides and my mouth went dry, all in preparation to run, fight, or in my case, save the day.

My body badly needed rest and, yet, I was not able to rest. But I kept doing the job I was good at for many more years than was healthy for me, because my nervous system was locked in a rigid mode of survival.

Reflecting on this is helpful for me. I like to look at what I've learned and how everything and everyone in my life continues teaching me how to be more whole. Funny, I'm not so good at a crazy pace anymore. Sure, it's age and maybe even some wisdom, but mostly I am just happy that I've found the slower gear to use when I want to. I'm getting good at that, too.

PART III

NOTHING'S
FOR NOTHING

The Inconvenience of Caring

My Mom had a stroke at a very inconvenient time in my life. I was in the middle of legal proceedings to press charges on someone who'd been stalking me for the previous six months and I was having nightmares. My stomach was in knots. People I thought were my friends weren't there for me, not wanting to be involved, I guess, in the scary shit I'd gotten mixed up in with the ex-boyfriend stalker. I was emotionally exhausted, feeling defensive, edgy and very alone.

At the same time, I'd been preparing to take my acupuncture board exams, the culmination of a grueling four years of full-time school. To prepare for exams, I studied six or seven hours every day, while working nights and weekends teaching advanced first aid and CPR to pay my way. I was tired, burned out, too busy and not in the mood for this.

One afternoon I decided to interrupt my studying and dutifully gave Mom a call. She was impossible to talk to, never asked about me and my life, while incessantly droning on about her boring little escapades. She especially loved to tell me all about her latest doctor's appointment and how the doctor would never have guessed she was "her age." Gawd. Just kill me. I dialed her number, though, hoping it'd be brief.

But today, she didn't answer. I let it ring until her machine picked up, then left her a message. I tried again. She must be out shopping, I thought, or at another doctor's appointment, flirting like the 85-year-old teenager she was. I tried calling later on around dinnertime and still no answer.

My gut told me there was something wrong, so I called 911 and told them Mom wasn't answering her phone. Emergency services were prompt and got ahold of her building manager, who opened the door to find her unconscious. The police called me and said she wasn't breathing when they and the paramedics arrived and they were transporting her to the hospital. I caught the next ferry from Victoria to Vancouver.

At the emergency ward of Saint Paul's Hospital, Mom lay there like a deflated balloon, so pale, without her dentures or lipstick, like someone I didn't know. The doctor told me she likely wouldn't last the night. I struggled to feel something other than a petty annoyance and barely suppressed rage that she'd never been the mother I wanted or needed anyhow and here she was, fucking inconveniencing me again.

Mom's stroke was just the start of the inconvenience and gut-wrenching battles for us both over the next three years of my caring for her, enduring her tirades and trying to find it in me to keep coming back day after day. Mom's sister, my Aunt Dot, told me, "She never was much of a mother to you, but in the end, you taught her." Not entirely true.

The real truth is that through our struggles together, Mom taught me how to make love a priority over everything else. My selfishness and resentment were right out there in plain sight for me to see and that started to change me.

Mom and I learned a lot together in those last years. What I thought at the time was inconvenience turned out to be the thing I needed most. The inconvenience of Mom's stroke was what it took for me to learn the most valuable lesson: how to care and be a good daughter and a better person.

There for Her

Shortly after Mom had her stroke in 2005, I arranged to have her moved from Vancouver to Victoria, where I lived, so I could visit her in the extended-care hospital and advocate for her. Mom had been active and very healthy her whole life and now at age eighty-five she was bedridden, paralyzed and irate. From the time she'd regained consciousness after the stroke, Mom was on a tirade, screaming, thrashing, swearing and lashing out at anyone in her path.

She was hell on wheels.

I found a facility in Victoria that had an opening, so I had Mom brought over by ambulance on the ferry from Vancouver. I was there to meet her and as soon as they rolled her in on the gurney and when she saw where she was, Mom began demanding to go back home to her little subsidized apartment in Vancouver's West End.

"What the fuck is with all you people? Take me home right now you bastards!"

Even the seasoned nurses and care aides at the new extended-care home looked a little scared and wide-eyed, trying and failing with the usual methods to calm down an agitated patient. Mom's screams and curses echoed through the halls, so they had to move her from the ward to a private room and at that point, even though I knew how scared and confused she was, I still just felt embarrassed and resentful.

After a few weeks, Mom's tantrums were less frequent and mostly ignored by the staff, so she saved all her anger for when I'd visit, hurling whatever she felt like saying straight at me. The stroke had opened a flood gate of pent-up anger, which now just poured out.

One kind doctor, seeing how it was going with Mom coming to her new "home," explained that with strokes on the right side of the brain, the patient often has a "change" in demeanor. "Sometimes a stroke will turn an ornery person sweet and sometimes it's just the opposite," he offered. "Is this out of character for your mom to behave this way?" he asked.

"Not really" I told him. "She's always been a royal bitch."

I did my best to shine it on and not be affected by her wrath, but I really was shocked and crushed from being the recipient of such raw anger. I just grit my teeth though, and tried not to feel anything so I could keep going. I didn't know how else to cope...

Our relationship was tense from so many years of unspoken hurts and I knew moving her to Victoria was not going to be easy, but because Mom had alienated everyone else in her life at that point, I was the only one left to step up and take care of her. She regularly blamed me for "dragging" her away from her beloved Vancouver and there were never any thanks for my efforts to help her recover, which at first I was sure was possible.

I'd just finished four years of Chinese medicine school, where we were shown how acupuncture and herbs were used in hospitals in China as therapies to help neurological conditions like stroke and traumatic brain injury. I talked to my teachers at school and we created a treatment plan for Mom, which if done early, had a very good chance of giving her back mobility and other functions. I figured it was worth a try.

Mom's doctors gave me permission to add herbal formulas to the medications they gave her, and I was able to come and do a complicated protocol of scalp acupuncture with electric stimulation on my daily visits. I also arranged for Mom to take part in physical therapy sessions held once a week at a "stroke group" with other people in her condition. I was pretty sure it was all going to work and she would be able to go back to something of a normal life.

I was pretty sure I'd cure her, be her hero and she'd finally love me.

For a while she let me treat her with acupuncture and for a while she let me take her to the stroke group, where we did classes with about twenty other people. The physical therapists were wonderful, guiding us through movements with the unaffected side and then encouraging the paralyzed side to move with manual help.

I'd sit beside Mom and lift her flaccid left arm or leg around while she'd cuss at me under her breath in frustration and embarrassment. Mom was ashamed of her condition and now she'd become one of "those sick people" who she'd so often sneered at. One time she asked me, "What did I do to deserve this?" Then after a few weeks, to my great disappointment, Mom refused to go back to stroke group and told me not to do acupuncture anymore.

"Mom, I can't believe you're giving up. Don't give up. You can get better!"

"No. I can do this on my own. I don't need anyone's help. I can just do it myself. I don't want to be one of those crippled people. I'm going to get up. Fuck all of you."

But she never did. Mom hated to depend on anyone and being in this condition was the worst thing she could imagine because now she was completely dependent.

Looking back at some of our visits, I cringe at the pointless discussions with Mom telling me to "call a fucking cab" so she could "get out of this hellhole," with me yelling back in exasperation.

"Mom! You can't even walk! How can you take a cab?"

It seemed like a whole lifetime was being condensed into those three years Mom was in the hospital, with both of us so bitter and unhappy, both wanting to blame the other for our hurts and losses. I dreaded our visits and yet also somehow cherished having this time we'd never gotten when I was growing up. The intensity of those months, with just the two of us, turned out to be one of the greatest blessings for us both.

It was necessary for us to yell our way through some of it and cry our way through some of it in order to process the grief and loss of what we'd never been able to share together when I was a child. And there were soft times, too, like on nice days, when she'd ask me to take her outside to the courtyard vegetable gardens. I'd push her wheelchair around, with her pointing to plants, asking to smell and taste things, noticing when a plant needed water or propping up and ordering me to do so, which I did gladly. Those were sweet times that still make me smile.

What I'd hoped for most was for Mom to rally and live the rest of her days with us loving one another, doing things together, as mother and daughter, making up for lost time and healing all the pain...

But she didn't fight for her life like I expected her to do. It made me furious and broke my heart. I didn't understand it because Mom was always someone who reveled and indulged in life's sensual pleasures. She loved sunshine, black coffee, hamburgers, wind in her hair, walking in the rain, laughing, dancing, playing her piano. She loved men, flirting, lipstick, perfume, racy movies and slinky clothes. And she loved swimming, the beach and fish and chips…

I expected her to fight. I wanted her to fight to live again. I wanted more time with her at the beach, to finally love and feel loved by her. I will never fully understand her choice to just gradually let go. I don't have to understand her journey and now it only counts that I have no regrets, because I was there for her.

LOVING ANYONE HELPS —— US LOVE EVERYONE ——

I didn't feel good about myself for many years. Because I was so insecure and wounded, I didn't know how to be a good friend or how to make a strong friendship. Basically, I was so scared to commit to anything or anyone that I sabotaged all of my relationships by taking the easy, selfish way out every time.

I couldn't even commit to an appointment or plans for something, because it felt suffocating to me, as if my future was "closed in." My behavior made it hard for people to trust me and rely on me and then I'd feel more isolated and get more "evidence" that I was just no good.

I wasn't honest either, because I was always trying to hide what I felt, and then I'd have to hide the shame of those feelings. It was a lot of work to keep running from myself and I remember my mouth feeling dry and my heart pounding with fear at what next obstacle I'd have to encounter. I wasn't comfortable in my own skin and no matter how hard I tried to keep on with what I had been doing for so many years, I never felt like I was doing anything right.

People say you have to hit rock bottom to change, but it's more complicated than that. You may already be on rock bottom and still nothing has changed and besides, there might be an even lower bottom you haven't hit yet. So what changes our course when we are on a path of destruction?

Maybe the answer is easier than we believe it to be. Maybe the answer is caring. Caring is what changes us, starting with caring for ourselves. Caring is what changes others. When we care we are changed. When we care about someone or something, we change. There are lots of ways to show it.

Loving anyone helps us love everyone. It's a start anyhow.

Being Seen

Being seen is how we know we exist, how we connect with one another. When we express joy, sadness, grief, disappointment, rage, love, excitement, triumph, despair…and when these expressions are reflected back to us, we feel our roots shoot down into the earth, anchoring us to humanity. We have a deep, mortal need to be seen. Being seen is integral to feeling human, and integral to feeling a part of something like family.

Seeing someone without projecting what we believe about them is a learned skill. We learn to acknowledge presence by having someone else acknowledge us. That way we get to feel what it's like to be regarded. It is a generous, life-affirming gift.

We also learn how not to give attention to or ignore someone, because of how we did not get attention we needed early in life. Neglect can desiccate one's soul. We humans know that isolation is the worst kind of punishment. Prisons use isolation to crush spirits and no good ever comes of it.

When my dad was mad at me, he'd pointedly ignore any attempts to communicate with him. Nothing I said or did was registered. If I asked for something, or even if I fell and skinned my knee, he would give no response.

Predictably, the stories he'd told me of "getting the silent treatment" from his mother if he didn't "do her bidding" were now being played out in how he related to his children.

I'd panic and implode, feeling like I didn't exist, desperate to atone for my sin. That was the desired effect. The isolation of not being seen, or at least my sense of it, was a way to control me, to show me that I really had no power at all, unless my father acknowledged my existence.

The deepest of all wounds are often the most subtle.

Even then, I knew my dad was trying to communicate to me how deeply whatever I had done had hurt him. Yet, in his attempt to punish me, I think the separation caused him even more pain than it did me. We were both wounded...

Mom had a way of just not listening to me, so that I'd wonder if she even heard me when I spoke.

"Hey Mom, I just got an award for teaching!" I told her excitedly.

"I have to get some more lipstick at London Drugs," she said absently, like she hadn't been listening. "I like the pink one I got last time. Everyone says I look the best in pink."

"Mom, did you hear me? I was just saying that I got an award for teaching. It's really cool that Saint John Ambulance recognizes my teaching there for the past twenty years."

"Oh, that's nice. Let's go to the drugstore now."

In this way, we were not able to develop intimacy. We kept missing each other in our communication. I felt unseen, and yet, because I never voiced it to her, afraid of furthering the distance I felt, the issue never got addressed. I'd try to give her a kiss and my lips would always graze her cheek, as she turned away.

That's how our communication went, forever missing the mark.

Mom would talk about growing up in what sounded like an idyllic childhood, with lots of siblings, in a big house in Maritime Canada, but under it all, not being seen was what she remembered most.

"My mother was a society lady, always busy with her meetings and paintings. We were raised by the servants," Mom would tell me wistfully.

"She'd pinch my cheeks to make them red, before company came, so I'd look pretty. And my dad was a physician and surgeon. He was very busy, too. I had to cut my finger for him to pay attention to me."

Now, years later, I see how both my parents had parents who didn't bond with their children in some critical way. Neither my mother nor my father had felt seen by their parents, so they were unable to nurture one another and were also unable to nurture their children with the loving attention they had never received themselves.

Our experiences become beliefs and beliefs can be projected onto the world, to become our reality. Without healing old beliefs, the lens we look through is distorted with pain.

I read an article recently about lasting relationships and how sharing sorrow and joy with another is what really bonds us. Listening, responding, giving the gift of our attention, allows someone to feel seen, regarded, important. And that feeling, over and over again, is what creates bonds that last.

As Adyashanti, one of my favorite spiritual teachers, says: "What we give our time and attention to is what grows in our experience."

At the end with Mom, when she was in her last days, she started listening to me, sharing my joy and sorrow, looking into my eyes. This didn't happen overnight, but when it was just the two of us, with nothing else to distract from the moment, the dust began to settle.

Lots of old unfinished business was just sitting there, ripe for the picking, so we thrashed through all that had been unsaid, all there'd been "no time" to talk about. Now there was nothing but time to feel it, say it.

And it was pretty brutal some times. I often left there crying, again feeling the familiar stab of not being seen.

One day I was there with her, talking about my work and the different careers I've had. I told her I finally felt like I was doing what I really wanted with my acupuncture and counseling practice.

Reaching out, brushing the hair from my face, she said to me, "You are a special person. I am proud of you."

It's one of my favorite things I ever heard from Mom. Hearing her say that let me know she was healing her own hurt and sharing that healing with me. We were both being seen.

☯

····· I AM ·····

When we feel a strong emotion we often say: "I am mad." "I am afraid." "I am happy." We say "I am" because the feeling can be all encompassing, so we feel as though "we are" the feeling. Yet, there is something in us noticing our emotion. What is that which notices? Am I that too? What or who am I?

Even when we are experiencing strong and difficult emotions, there is always something in us noticing and we may even sense a calm "eye of the storm" quietly witnessing. Is what notices who we actually are? Am I that silent, calm awareness? Or am I the strong, difficult emotion? Who am I?

Spiritual teacher Adyashanti says to notice "the you who is having no difficulty, even when you are having difficulty." This may sound like nonsense at first, even contradictory, because Zen-like teachings are like riddles. But even so, you might have felt the sense of awareness, and a neutral kind of observation which can arise even in some of your most difficult moments.

These lucid flashes of awareness may come as insight, clarity or answers to the questions of what to do or not do. Trauma and difficulties in life can actually transform us in ways we never expected. When things are tough and we move through them, a unique perspective opens up.

Maybe there is a whole universe of lightness available and I am

*just so bound up in my own inner world that I forget to notice
what is much bigger than me.*

*Am I both the one having difficulty and the one noticing
that I am having difficulty? Something in me remembers silence.
Silence remembers silence. Am I silence?*

. . . .

Bullying

Scratch the surface of any person who bullies and you will
find someone who has been bullied. Nonviolent Communication
pioneer Marshall Rosenberg says, "Everything we do is in service of
our needs." So what possible need could someone bullying another
person be trying to fulfill? What could someone who is behaving
hurtfully and exerting power over another be trying to communicate
other than, "I'm stronger than you"?

Because I had no mother at home, my dad would brush my long,
tangled hair and tie it up into two crooked pony tails to get me ready
for school. We were poor and I wore a weird combination of church
hand-me-downs and my older brother's clothes. We had a lot of cats
and our house wasn't clean, so I didn't smell great either.

One older girl picked me out to bully every day. She called me,
"Dusty, because your hair is ugly, you stink like sour milk and pee
and your leotards have cat fur stuck all over them." I was always
shocked when she'd speak to me that way and when she punched me
and pushed me into puddles, I'd go home crying.

My dad, for all his faults, knew what it was to be bullied and he'd
tell me, "Just ignore her, Honey. She's just jealous of you because
you're a nice person. Be kind to the kids who others are mean to.
You'll see. You're going to be fine."

The girl stopped bullying me eventually. I think it might have been because she could see that in spite of my funny hair and bad smell, I had friends. In time, my bully became my friend and protector, too. I wondered if it was true that she actually felt jealous of me, but it didn't matter. I was just happy she wasn't mad at me anymore.

My guess is that the girl was bullied herself, maybe at home. Why did she behave like she did? I wonder if she was somehow trying to communicate how lonely and isolated she felt. I wonder if she was seeking empathy by showing how she was treated. "I will show you how it feels to be hurt so I can be understood, so you will care." Maybe that was how what she was doing was in service of her needs…

And maybe there is a little of this in all of us, this need for empathy, which gets twisted into something uncaring and punitive.

Advocate

When Mom had her massive stroke and had to live in a nursing home, she was mad as hell. She swore, kicked and punched, even spit at anyone within range. Though I understood her frustration, rage and grief, there were plenty of times I wanted to walk away and never come back.

But I had to come back, because no one else would. She was the only Mom I had, so I was her advocate, charged with making sure she was cared for properly.

I knew my role and I knew the lessons I was learning from her about being gracious (because she wasn't) and kind (because she was an awful bitch to everyone) and fighting for her precious life… which she didn't do. She gave up on trying and instead cursed each day she had to endure.

And that broke my heart. I didn't understand why all that vitriol couldn't be channeled into her recovery, rather than to shake her fist each day at God for, as Mom put it, "punishing" her.

As an acupuncturist, I'd worked with people recovering from brain injuries, both traumatic and non-traumatic, like the stroke that caused Mom's paralysis. I'd personally witnessed my patients and others recover some or all of their original function, with daily acupuncture, physical therapy and a willingness to work hard.

I tried everything I could, but she didn't want my help.

Mom used to play her old upright piano every day and fancied herself a songwriter who'd one day make it big in Nashville. Naturally, I thought she'd be excited for me to roll her down the hall to a side room near the cafeteria, where there was a big old upright, just waiting to be played.

"Look Mom," I said, pushing her wheelchair into the room. "Here's a piano for you and you can play it anytime you want."

"Take me out of here! And don't you touch it. You can't play!" She shrieked.

So we went back to her room, where she stared at the wall, full of childish rage and grief. The crushing loss of freedom strangled her will to recover. Days, weeks and months went by and Mom began complaining about one of her nurses, saying she was "too rough" when handling her.

I spoke with the nurse carefully, not wanting to offend. "My Mom says she's feeling a little sore these days and so wanted me to ask you and the other nurses to be extra gentle with her."

The nurse nodded and smiled and since I knew my Mom was not the sweet little old lady she appeared to be (rather, having a foul temper and a mouth like a sailor), I cut the nurse some slack and thanked her for putting up with Mom.

The next time I came there, Mom was red faced and thrashing about at the nurses, calling them "a bunch of stupid cunts" as they and the care aids tried to get her off the commode and back into bed.

"They locked me in a room by myself for hours! Those bitches just locked me away like I was a criminal!"

"What?" I asked the nurse who was rushing out of the room, "What happened? Did my mother get locked up? Is this true?"

Stone-faced, the nurse told me "You mother is a very difficult patient. She was yelling and making too much noise so we temporarily put her in the visitor's room across the hall."

"I see. I'll be speaking with the head nurse at our next care meeting to discuss this," I growled, barely containing my anger.

The nurses left us alone and Mom sobbed with little gasps, like a child, hiding her face from me. I sat on the bed and began to kiss her cheeks and brush her hair, rocking her and singing the only song I could think of, the one I'd sung to her many years before, as a three-year-old:

"Robin in the rain, what a saucy fellow.
Robin in the rain, mind your socks of yellow.
Running in the garden with your nimble feet, looking for your dinner with your long, strong beak.
Robin in the rain, you don't mind the weather.
Showers always make you gay. But the worms are wishing that you would stay at home.
Robin on a rainy day..."

It was the first time she'd let me soothe her. She closed her eyes and hummed as I sang, tapping her fingers on the sheet, allowing my touch.

Daughter became mother.

The following week I arrived early and got Mom dressed, put some pink lipstick on her and rolled her wheelchair down the hall to attend the monthly "care team meeting," where patients and family meet with nurses and other staff for patient-care updates.

Mom's face was greasy with tension, like she was going to trial, and I draped a protective arm around her shoulder as charts and medications were reviewed by the head nurse. At one point, it was looking like the meeting was almost over, but no one had asked Mom or me if we wanted to speak.

I introduced myself and started, "I know that nursing is a hard job and I know that sometimes patients are not the easiest."

Mom giggled nervously and flashed a goofy smile to charm the room and show everyone how adorable and friendly she was.

"Ahem. Well, anyhow, my Mom is unhappy with one of her nursing aids and I would like to request that she not have that care provider working with her any longer."

"Ah, well that won't be possible to change the shifts around," the nurse interrupted. "Unfortunately, patients don't get to choose..."

I cut her off.

"And I would like that staff member reprimanded for locking my mother in a room across the hall alone, with no call bell. Is that standard procedure around this place?"

The room was silent.

"Of course isolating patients is not standard procedure and your mother will not have that care aid on her wing again. We are very sorry that she had to endure such a thing."

"You can apologize to her then. She's paying your salary."

"Mrs. Smith," Nurse Ratchet stuttered, "We are very sorry for what happened and it won't happen again. Please accept our sincere apologies."

Mom nodded and squeezed my hand as we rolled out of the room along the shiny-tiled hallway.

"We sure showed those fuckers, eh?" Mom said through a giggle.

"Yes Mom, we sure did."

My Conversion

I grew up going to church a lot, every Sunday morning and night, Wednesday evenings for Crusaders (the Pentecostal church's answer to girl guides) and also Friday-night service. Going to church so often was supposed to keep us kids out of trouble, which didn't work so well with me in the long run. I only learned that I didn't want to be there and didn't believe what I was being told.

The only thing I really liked was the singing, when everyone seemed to be as one voice, and I also loved it when my dad played his harmonica for the congregation. I was in the choir and got to do solos sometimes, too, and since I am a natural ham, I enjoyed that the most.

I was a precocious child and learned to say all sixty-six books of the bible by the age of three, with their tongue-twisting names like "Zephaniah" and "Haggai." My dad, taking his turn as assistant pastor for the day, would prop his toddler up on the pulpit and I'd proudly recite each and every one in a little song I was taught. The crowd always went wild and I have a vivid memory of what it was like to feel I'd done something "right."

Church was never something that nurtured my spirit, though, the way I'd heard people talk about it. I was never baptized nor felt like I'd been "born again" or "saved." I stopped going when I turned twelve, seeing only the hypocrisy between what people said and how they lived their lives and how they treated one another. I always felt bad after church, like I was forever burdened with the incurable disease of sin, never to be redeemed until after death, maybe.

Many years later, when I was in my forties, I went for the first time to Catholic mass. I had no expectations and also, after all those years, I'd even forgotten my cynical fear of religion that might block what I experienced. Sitting quietly during the liturgy, a deep pool of silence and peace began welling up in my chest, bringing tears to my eyes.

Looking around the cathedral, I sensed a gathering of many different people, all with a common passion. I can't explain how or why I became enraptured and saw visions of tiny "flames" above the heads of the congregation, but each person reflected joy straight into my heart, igniting a long-forgotten memory of complete contentment.

I kept going back to mass often, several times a week, but it was my choice this time and I was being nurtured. I was ready for something to change in my life.

If I have ever "sinned" it has been against myself, not God or Jesus or some other thing outside of me. My sins have been all the times I neglected to honor the still, quiet and wise place in my soul that knows what is true and what is an illusion. I turned away from myself and therefore, in the purest sense, I turned away from the oneness of God.

I decided that right now was the best time for me to have a "do over" for my soul, which was my secret way of thinking of my conversion, so I spoke to the priest, Father John, about converting. He looked at me sternly, "You will have to attend eight months of Catholicism classes each Wednesday night."

"Yes. I will do that. Thank you!" I said, smiling all the way home and wondering if I was crazy, while at the same time, feeling I was following an important instinct, very personal to me.

I faithfully attended the eight months of catechism classes, always being the one who'd speak up with my opinions and disagreements about Catholic dogma, much to the sideways glances of all the nice church ladies working so hard to convert my sinner's soul. But in spite of my rebellion, one day Father John told me I was ready and soon could be baptized on Holy Saturday, the day before Easter Sunday.

I wore my best dress, a long red one, which seemed appropriate for me. I convinced a few friends to attend the service, too. Even if they didn't understand and thought it was strange, I still wanted someone I knew to witness the moment my sins were all forgiven and I was once and for all getting a fresh start.

All I really remember was the moment water was poured over my brow, as Father John prayed to dedicate my soul to heaven. A rush of light to my head almost knocked me over and the two attendants on my arms steadied me, as I stood to face the congregation, all smiling and applauding their welcome of me into the family of saints.

The next morning was a blessed, sunny Easter Sunday and I put on a blue dress, walking to mass with a light heart. Father John smiled broadly at me, people shook my hand and hugged me. I did feel part of a family, though not one of saints, but rather a family of forgiveness of all I'd ever believed I did wrong. Sitting there during Easter mass, it dawned on me that my conversion was a celebration, a shedding of belief that I was ever anything but perfect.

The bishop was at mass that day, too, and was offering to perform the sacrament of confession afterwards. I was excited to at last, as a real Catholic, get a chance to confess my sins. The bishop, having been present at my baptism service the night before, looked wide-eyed, as I walked into the room.

"But my dear, what are you doing here?" he asked.

"I would like to confess." I said, trying not to be too excited.

"But my dear, you are without sin. You have just been washed clean. You are pure, like a newborn baby. Please, just leave today and give your smile to someone on the street as a gift from God. Go now and sin no more."

I left without a confession that day and, honestly, I never have confessed. I'm still basking in the letting go of all that I thought was wrong with me and accepting that I am perfect, just like everyone else is and always has been. It took me a while to believe it and I forget sometimes, too...

But it's only ever been between me and God anyhow.

THE YANG OF
····· CHRIST RISING ·····

Today is Easter Sunday and I've been musing about how Christianity and Taoism have much more in common than we think. Christian doctrine says that on Easter Sunday, Jesus rose from the dead, out of the tomb, into the light.

Taoists note how springtime is the most yang season, when everything comes out of dormancy, rising to the sky with new growth. From what seems like the darkness and death of winter, emerges a miracle of life. Yang force surges upward, pushing through the density, revealing the always present light.

Yang brightness springs from yin darkness. The seed reveals its sprout.

Christ gestates in the stillness and silence of the tomb and is born anew.

In Taoist philosophy, the concepts of Yin and Yang and the Five Elements are at the heart of traditional Chinese medicine (tcm). Like the Yin/Yang symbol, with one side white and the other black, and each side with a circle of the opposite shade in it, nothing is absolutely one way or another. Within all that is Yang (forceful, hot, external, masculine) there also exists some Yin (gentle, cool, internal, feminine)... One is summer and the other is winter; one is night and the other day; yet both are constantly, dynamically moving and changing.

The five elements of wood, fire, earth, metal and water are part of a complex system used for diagnosis and prescription of acupuncture points, as well as herbal medicine, diet, lifestyle and other Chinese medical therapies.

The wood element is related to spring, the color green, sour taste and anger. Springtime is the most yang season of the year, because all the force built up over the dormant winter months just bursts forth.

Growing up as a preacher's kid I became thoroughly steeped in Christian doctrine, and over the last decade, studying and practicing Chinese medicine, nearly everything I see is through an East Asian lens and how I think has become a blend of both disciplines. Easter, therefore, is more than a Christian tradition to me. The richness of history and culture honors and points to more than we know.

As the story goes, when Christ was nailed to a wooden cross, given sour vinegar to drink, he released his anger to God. "Why hast thou forsaken me?" Then Jesus evolved through his pain. "Forgive them, they know not what they do." From Yang to Yin and into the alchemical blackness of the tomb, his agony processed into gold.

There's a timeless parallel between the darkness of the tomb, the darkness of winter and the rising of Christ from the dead, like a daffodil springing out from a dry, dead bulb under the soil.

Whenever I've gone to Easter mass, my favorite part is when the symbolic body of Christ is held high and we're all supposed to repeat, "Lord, I am not worthy to receive you. Only say the word, and I shall be healed."

Problem is, I believe just the opposite. Is that wrong?

Under all the fear, grief, anger, regret and belief that I was bad and unworthy, the light in me has been gestating, fertilized by the muck of my despair, feeding dormant seeds of wisdom and resiliency.

Through the darkness, light pulls us forward, like the seedling, like Christ rising. We can try to resist, but nature keeps moving and renewing us, because we are nature. She always gets the last word.

. . . .

Who's In There

A few years ago I visited my family on Prince Edward Island, Canada's smallest province, tucked away on the frigid Eastern Seaboard. My ancestors emigrated there two-hundred-and-fifty years ago from Ireland, arriving to a wild land of wind and sky, where they eked out a simple existence from the sea. Even now, hundreds of years later, life and the people are much the same.

One of the first things I noticed was how people tried to catch my eye when I walked by them. Unlike the big cities, where most folks try their best to avoid eye contact, here in Charlottetown, PEI, every person I walked past seemed to be making a special effort to look me in the face. At first I thought it was just the men flirting, then I saw the women, kids, old folks, too, all taking the time to look into my eyes as they passed.

With all the visiting, eating and touristy outings, I never said anything to any of my family, for fear they'd think me strange for mentioning what had become a big question mark in my mind. Just why were those people all looking at me? Was it something I was wearing? Was there something wrong with how I was conducting myself?

I decided to pay close attention, the next time we were out and about, just to see for myself what it was that people were looking at. I'd been uncomfortable with looking at them myself, the way they were so intently looking at me, because my sister had told me long ago that to look in a stranger's eyes would be taken as a challenge, so now I felt a little paranoid.

This was different, though, because it was everyone who was looking and, yes, they were looking right into my eyes when we were in a store, restaurant or even just passing on the street. It wasn't a challenge. I could tell that people were peering into me, to see who I was. They were curious and at the same time, their look said, "I see you. I welcome you."

That night at dinner with all the aunts, uncles and cousins, I spoke up and started telling everyone my epiphany about the mysterious glances of maritime strangers. "At first I thought there was something wrong with me and that's why they were all looking," I said. "Then I noticed how warm and friendly those looks were."

"Of course," Aunt Jean said, "That's how we are here. When we look at you we are trying to see who's in there. It's a compliment to be regarded like that, eh?"

Yes. Why yes it is.

— ANXIETY AND CORTISOL —

Many people wake up feeling anxious. One reason is because cortisol, the hormone our adrenal glands produce and secrete when we feel stress, is highest at the start of the day. Cortisol ramps up early in the morning to get us going and tapers off at bedtime, but we can become anxious if we have an excess of cortisol in our bloodstream, without a way to discharge it. And, the catch is, the more anxious we are, the more cortisol we produce. Ack!

Cortisol does lots of things, including working to stop inflammation and helping us mobilize resources to fight or flee from danger. Normal ups and downs of this hormone can be expected but we produce inordinate amounts of it when we are stressed for extended periods. Chronic stress pumps up the anxiety…and, well, you know the rest.

When I've been on autopilot and not taking care of myself by resting and having enough "down time" to recover, my body says NO! And I get a signal, like insomnia or waking up anxious, that tells me that I need to pay attention to my thoughts, which drive emotions, which drive my nervous system, which controls EVERYTHING in my body.

Finding ways to discharge pent up energy and reset is an essential part of self-care. Start by checking in with yourself and take some deep breaths. Even that will help a lot if it becomes a habit when stress comes up.

Thank You /
I'm Sorry / I Love You

These three things are difficult to say when we are defending ourselves. "Thank you" means: You gave me something that made a difference to me; I let myself appreciate you; I see that you are extending yourself to me. "I'm sorry" means: I humbly notice that something I have done has hurt you; I want to make amends; please forgive me so I can forgive myself. "I love you" means: my heart wants to connect more deeply with you; I care for who you are and I feel nourished in your presence; you are important to me.

I talk about my Mom a lot because I learned so many lessons with her, especially in our last few years together. She fled the violence of our family home when I was quite young and because of this we'd had challenges trying to piece together a mother/daughter relationship over the years. Mom had never said those three things to me: thank you, I'm sorry, I love you.

After she had her stroke and was in the hospital, each day I'd visit her and before leaving I'd try to kiss her on the forehead and tell her I loved her, though I'd never get a kiss or an "I love you" back. When I left I'd usually cry on the way home, feeling sad, resentful and exhausted.

"I love you Mom." Sometimes I kind of choked on those words to her wondering why I even tried. Saying "I love you" when I had never heard that from my mother felt unnatural, but I said it anyhow, because I wanted to actually feel it and wanted to hear her say it even more. It was especially hard for me to say "I love you" since during our visits, she'd yell and curse at me, venting her frustration and rage on the only one who'd take it, day after day.

"Taking it" day after day was burning me up inside and I could feel the all too familiar resentment and powerlessness that'd been with me my whole life. I wanted something from her and I was trading my soul for it. I wanted her love so badly that I was willing swallow the pain, walk on eggshells, do anything to feel her love and acceptance.

During a particularly agonizing session with my counselor Margaret, I wailed, "I can never do enough for her. She never approves of me. She fucking yells at me and calls me names when I'm the only person who even visits her. She hates me! All I want is for her to just fucking love me!"

Margaret let me get it all out and then said, "Maybe you don't need to keep 'taking it' from your mom. If you are hurt by what she says, maybe you can give yourself permission to let her know you feel hurt."

"I can't do that! She will yell more. She will never let me close. She will never love me!"

"I guess you have to decide if you are willing to risk your fear of what might happen by standing up for yourself. You might even be surprised."

My stomach flipped with just thinking of my next visit with Mom. Now that I'd admitted to myself how battered I felt, just trying to "muscle my way through," I could see how doing that was a very old pattern of self-violence. I'd learned how to ignore my feelings and shove aside the pain and now I was faced with an opportunity to do something totally different.

It'd been more than two years since her stroke and a lifetime of believing I was not worthy of her love and when Mom began to yell at me again that day, every cell in my body seemed to freeze, but I got up anyhow and said, "I'm sorry Mom. I have to leave now. I feel hurt when you speak that way to me so I'm going, but I'll be back tomorrow. I love you." Mom yelled and screamed as I walked out of her hospital room. Guilt sat in my guts like a stone and something else I couldn't recognize was there too, like very small, soft, open, breeze in my chest.

For months, when I'd return to visit, Mom cried and refused to look at me, showing her displeasure that I'd not put up with her behavior and had chosen to leave. I'd give her a couple of minutes to change her mind about starting another tantrum, but she'd usually start getting agitated and begin yelling, and sometimes even spitting at me. So I would have to leave again, doing the same as before, stating why I was leaving, telling her "I love you," trying to land a kiss on her forehead if I could.

Those were some of the hardest times for us. I understood her childish rage at being left behind, because I'd felt that very thing most of my life. Mom was my perfect mirror.

And I kept standing up when she became abusive, telling her she was hurting my feelings with her words, saying, "I love you and I'll be back tomorrow." The important part was keeping my promise and coming back the next day. I needed to do this for both of us, for me to learn how to be dependable and for her to trust me, depend on me.

Each visit I did the same thing, drawing a boundary for what I would tolerate, always trying to give her a chance to change her mind and actions. I was sick with worry, still wondering if I risked further distance from her by saying 'no' to her outbursts. Some days I went home and threw up from sheer panic that I was making things worse, yet I could feel a strength growing in me and a small voice said, "Keep going."

Some days were better than others when I'd visit her. It wasn't always completely horrible and there were even moments I'd catch Mom looking at me, wistfully, tenderly, but not speaking in those ways. It was how her face softened and I'd catch a glimpse of her loving me, despite the spiteful words that tumbled out of her.

On those days, I'd also cry on the way home, but from gratitude, strong in my new found conviction that something important was happening for us both.

And one day I walked in to see her. The day before had been particularly harsh, with Mom throwing things, swearing at the top of her lungs, screaming and wailing at me to "Leave and never come back!"

It'd been so traumatic that one of the nurses called me at home to see if I was okay. "I heard your mom today and I know that must be very hard for you. If you don't mind me saying so, she is a real piece of work and she is lucky to have you."

After the call I stayed there on the couch, feeling a swirl of emotions spinning in my chest. That night I dreamed of Mom, falling off a wall, like Humpty Dumpty and me sobbing, trying to piece her together again…

It was Sunday and I rode my bike to the care home to see her. Walking in and removing my helmet, I saw Mom sitting up in bed. Her famous fluffy hair, which she'd let go flat and matted at the back, was backcombed into a 1950ish bouffant. She wore a pink sweater, light pink lipstick and smelled like her favorite perfume, Red Door.

"Hi Mom," I ventured. "You look pretty today."

"Hello Rebekah dear. Please sit down," she said sweetly.

"Rebekah, I want to say I'm sorry for speaking to you the way I have. Thank you for visiting me all this time, when I've been so terrible. I love you. You are my beautiful daughter. I love you."

"Oh Mom, I love you too. I love you, I love you, I love you…"

And that's how it was for the rest of our time together. We made up for all the "I love yous" that had never been said. We stared into one another's eyes, saying over and over again, "I love you. I love you. I love you."

During those last few months together, all of our visits were full of, "thank you, I love you, I'm sorry for hurting you." Mostly we just said, "I love you."

And when a series of strokes finally put Mom into a coma, I spent a precious week lying in bed next to her, my head on her heart, her fingers in my hair, listening to each ragged breath leaving her.

Our eyes met one last time and there I saw the entire universe expanding into nothingness. Mom left this world, unafraid, light as a feather and free as a bird.

── DEATH AND GRIEF ──

In our society, grief has become something we "get through" or "get over," rather than allowing pain and sadness to lead us on a path to wholeness. Teacher, storyteller and palliative care specialist Stephen Jenkinson speaks of death and grief in his award-winning film *Grief Walker*, as that which will change us when our hearts are broken open, after which we will never be the same. Too often, though, we resist change and try to cover up our sadness, vulnerability, helplessness and loneliness, missing the opportunity to experience our depths.

When Mom passed away, I only allowed myself three days off work. She'd conveniently died on a Friday, so I was back at work on Monday, hollow with grief, sobbing in the bathroom between patients, exhausted in my soul, yet trying to "get through it" so I could "get on with my life." I hadn't been kind to myself, hadn't given my heart a chance to feel the enormity of sadness.

After several weeks, I wrote something to express my grief of finally feeling Mom's love and then having to say goodbye too soon:

DNA stranded us
Together
Like this one
From my core
Stretched taut
By all the years
I willed
You
To Love
Me
Perpetual orbit
Around you

Burned me
Still I circled
Waiting to land
When one lurch forward
Tore
Our strands
Apart
Forever
Amazing me
With the breath
I take
Without
You

Once I got the words down, something began to relax. I allowed the softening to take me, without resisting. I'll never be the same.

"Everything is different now" – Don Henley

····· LUNG TIME ·····

As the last of summer slips away and the squash leaves *shrivel, the heat and moisture of late summer turns to the dryness of fall. Autumn is the season of the lungs, the element is metal, the color is white and the emotion is grief. The concept of grief fits for me in autumn. I feel a certain grief in letting go of the carefree summer days of bare feet and swimming, strawberries and raspberries off the vine and lying on the grass, soaking up hot, precious sunshine. Sigh. To everything there is a season.*

In Chinese medicine lung time is 3-5 am, the time of "Po," the corporeal soul and all things concerning the body and primal instincts. Po is affected by all emotions, especially worry, grief and sadness. When we indulge in these emotions deeply, without releasing the energy, it can cause an imbalance in the lungs' ability to take in all-important qi from the air we breathe.

The pair organ of the lungs is the large intestine, where we eliminate waste after our bodies use what is needed. Holding on to emotions can lead to constipation, which invites problems with the skin (like rashes) and toxins building up in the body.

The not-so-new science of psychoneuroimmunology is the biomedical study of how our thinking affects our nervous systems and, therefore, our immune and endocrine systems, too. This study of mind and body is intimately related to other healing modalities, such as East Asian, Ayurvedic and many other types of holistic medicine, always referring back to where the imbalance may have started. There is no doubt that what and how we think impacts more than just our minds, so finding ways to experience peace and calm is important to staying healthy.

. . . .

Margaret

I met Margaret when I really needed a friend. Margaret was a social worker and counselor, specializing in helping women who'd suffered violence and were experiencing post-traumatic stress. She only worked with women, she told me, "Because men have been the ones who've hurt the people I work with. It's my choice and I choose to work only with women."

After a dozen or so calls to counselors to ask if they'd take me on as a client and be paid later by the Province's Victims Services, Margaret was the only one to say, "Yes, of course I'd be happy to work with you." I was relieved and I liked the sound of her soft voice, with its English accent, which you hear a lot in Victoria.

In British Columbia's justice system, certain types of crimes are handled by the Crown Council, where charges are made by that judicial body against an individual, in order to protect the public. When I reported being stalked and harassed by a man, they asked me to document each occurrence and then proceeded to take action.

I hired a lawyer, who heard my story and kindly offered to help me, for just a small retainer. Thanks to the lawyer and a good friend who witnessed for me on the stand, I won my case, got a restraining order to keep me safe, and Victim's Services awarded me twenty-four months of weekly counseling sessions with Margaret to process all that I'd been through.

I'd had plenty of counseling work before. In fact, I have a counseling degree myself, specializing in post-traumatic stress so when it was me with the issues with post-traumatic stress, having the training to recognize it, helped me know I needed help from someone else.

A lot of memories were being dredged up from my teen years, when I lived on the street and felt alone and vulnerable. My childhood trauma resurfaced, even what I thought I'd dealt with and put to rest in all my years of therapy. But now I was strong enough to see even deeper into my pain and having a safe person to tell everything to brought me new peace and clarity.

There were days I'd drag myself into Margaret's office and just sob for the whole hour. I'd flop on her office couch, pouring my tears and wails into a pillow on her lap as she laid her hand on my back, soothing me, because that's the only thing either of us could do. Margaret knew she was mothering me for all the times I'd been a child and missed being held and her simple stability and loving kindness helped me gradually climb out of my pit of despair.

My Mom died during the time I was seeing Margaret and, because I'd had so many issues tied to my relationship with Mom, her illness and death were deeply transformative. I was so grateful to be able to tell Margaret every detail of my story about Mom. She listened patiently, asking me to say more, making sure I got out everything I needed to say even when our sessions were going overtime. She knew how important it was for me and as I sobbed through Mom's last moments and her beautiful letting go in love, Margaret cried with me in solidarity, joy and humanity.

I learned so much about how to be a better counselor from my work with Margaret and how to be a better friend, too. And though our relationship was a professional one, it is no less meaningful to me. Margaret's soulfulness is what allowed me to heal and integrate my pain, and you can't teach that at school. It has to come from the wise and experienced heart.

——— HYPERVIGILANCE ———

The habit of hypervigilance has faded for me over the years. I no longer panic when I'm anticipating meeting new people, fearing they will see all the holes in my psyche. I used to be so afraid of people seeing me, fearing I'd be judged, while at the same time I desperately wanted to be acknowledged and seen.

The hypervigilant mind and overactive nervous system has a primal instinct to hide weaknesses, the way a wounded animal does, in order to keep from being attacked. For so many years, I saw myself as a limping gazelle on the savanna, with lions all around. Nothing, nowhere and no one was safe.

The fear of people was strongest in me when I quit my crazy paramedic job, moved onto an old wooden boat and sailed up to Quadra Island to start a new life there, hoping to realize my dream of having a small piece of farm land to care for. I'd made the conscious choice to change my life and yet here in the grocery store on this quaint little island I was out of my mind with anxiety whenever I encountered another person.

And I'd always been so good with talking to people, so able to engage and be charming and fun. Now, though, I couldn't look people in the eye, my skin crawled with panic while I watched faces to see if they knew how much I just wanted to run away.

It didn't make sense at first, but I began to understand how, finally, my nervous system sensed I was somewhere safe enough to let down some of the defenses I'd depended on to survive, and that was somehow frightening. It reminds me of a quote from Jane Seabrook: "Please don't tell me to relax. It's only my tension that's holding me together." Letting down my guard was the most frightening thing. Trust was foreign. Hypervigilance was all I knew.

It happens often that people who have been homeless, addicted to drugs, assaulted or all of the above, receive housing or other help, and then have a very hard time adjusting to something other than what they have known for so long. It's hard to accept change when your nervous system has become fragile and brittle. Even when people mean well and want to help, the change is often too much to bear.

I remember how it was for me going into various foster homes, having decided long before that no one could be trusted. I was like an animal in a leg-hold trap, willing to chew off a limb rather than feel trapped again. I ran.

Then slowly, very slowly, here on Quadra I began to connect, first with animals, like my dog, cat, sheep, chickens, geese...I kept collecting critters on the small acreage we'd bought, where I'd hide in the long grass with them, just like I did when I was a kid in our backyard with my cats. A little corner of me felt safe with the animals and then that began to spread to feeling safe around people. I learned how to relax and not fall apart. My world started to open up.

I hardly recognize the terrified girl I was but I won't ever forget the icy feeling of fear, or how it felt when the ice began to thaw. I

*am not immune to fear and being triggered but I can stand back
and see it now, when it's happening, and that's a good thing. One
day at a time is how we heal. One thought, one breath at a time.
It's a whole new world out there.*

Face Value

Infants learn to read faces from the time they can see. Does
Mama care for me? Will she keep me safe? Will she feed me? Can I
depend on her? Even without language, the neurons are still firing
and what's seen in her face feels like a matter of life or death.

I used to wonder what was wrong with me when I was in my
twenties and thirties. I was so full of reckless anger, self-pity,
resentment, jealousy and bitterness, lots of bitterness.

Was there something I'd missed in my early moments with Mom?
Did I see in her face that she would be leaving soon? Did I see that
she was already detaching from me, protecting her own feelings? Was
that why I clung to her and at the same time pulled away?

When she left, I could never understand why she left without
me and my brother. Maybe she did the best she could by trying
to take us back once, but still, for over half my life, all I felt was
abandoned.

Years later after Mom died, I asked my therapist Margaret about
what I'd read on the importance of "the mother's loving gaze" of
adoration and unconditional love. I can't remember where I read it,
but it said something like: without the mother's loving gaze the child
is bereft, lacks proper brain chemistry development, will not thrive or
be able to bond in meaningful relationships.

I told her, "I don't think I got that loving gaze from my Mom.

That's why I've been so angry, so hopelessly lonely, such a total fuckup. I got ripped off. She had one foot out the door and just wanted to leave me. She didn't want me. I read it in her face."

"I know you believe you were deprived of something crucial," Margaret said. "You have been trying to make up for what you believe you didn't get by chasing connection in relationships, yet that hasn't helped, has it? Maybe something has been in the way of seeing and feeling your Mother's love.

"When your Mom was dying and you were there with her, what did you see in her face?"

The memory was fresh. Mom had just passed away a week before and I recalled everything about those last moments we shared. It'd been a soul-twisting three years of her illness for us both. We yelled and swore at each other. Mom hit me, spat at me and finally let me get close to her. And I let her close to me, finally. We both let down the walls of protection we'd built and held up since I was born.

"I saw in her face that she loved me with all of her heart. I saw how grateful she was that I was there with her and that it was just the two of us for the end of her life. I saw that she trusted me and thought I was the best person in the world. I saw in her face, in her eyes, that there was no one she'd rather have with her, because she'd always loved me."

I'd been telling myself a story all my life, just so I didn't have to confront my own anger and sadness at losing my Mom at such a young age. It was easier to believe that she didn't love me than to ache to be with her.

Her face was full of pain, but also full of love. Now I know.

ADDICTION
···· ROOT AND BRANCH ····

A few years back I co-presented a public talk with Dr. Gabor Maté, who was speaking about his renowned book on addiction, In the Realm of Hungry Ghosts, *and at one point, he invited me to speak about how East Asian medicine viewed addiction.*

I said, "The root of addiction is pain. The branch or manifestation of pain is addiction. Addiction cannot be healed by cutting the branches. Only getting to the root of pain, carefully, gently, patiently attending to it, will work to heal addiction."

In East Asian medicine, root and branch are treated at the same time. For instance, when someone has a digestive issue, we diagnose, then treat the symptoms (branches) and also treat the etiology or cause (roots) so that the patient not only feels better, but the disease can heal. Healing addiction requires holistic, soulful work using some or all things like: Harm reduction, Twelve-step programs, Detox, Counseling, Treatment programs aimed at not just abstinence, but deep inner exploration to heal the roots of pain.

In his book, Dr. Maté says: "Being cut off from our own natural self-compassion is one of the greatest impairments we can suffer. Along with our ability to feel our own pain go our best hopes for healing, dignity and love. What seems nonadaptive and self-harming in the present was, at some point in our lives, an adaptation to help us endure what we then had to go through. If people are addicted to self-soothing behaviors, it's only because in their formative years they did not receive the soothing they needed. Such understanding helps delete toxic self-judgment on the past and supports responsibility for the now, hence the need for compassionate self-inquiry."

We have a lot to learn as a society about how to care for one another. Compassion is the first step.

· ·

Drug Dreams

Every so often I wake up with my heart pounding, mouth dry and my nervous system in preparation to run or fight something. Then I realize I've been dreaming of some old memory. It seems so real and being back there again is the last place I want to be.

In my dreams I am a person who lies, cheats, steals, uses drugs and does anything to avoid being caught. In my dreams I am desperate, lonely, even physically violent and scared, always scared and running.

I try to run from my shame.

Throughout the dreams I am lost and when I try to call for help, no sound comes out. Or, more commonly, I have a phone, but I can't remember the number to call and more bad things keep happening... then I usually wake up in a sweat.

I've talked to addicts about these types of dreams, commonly called "drug dreams," which seem to come from nowhere, after a period of sobriety and lifestyle change.

One person was telling me, "Yeah, just when you start feeling like, 'Hey! I've got this,' then Bam! You dream you're right back there in the shit again. It's like a slap in the face. I dreamed I had the needle in my arm and when I woke up, at first I thought I might as well go get high. Then it sunk in that getting high didn't work before and it's not going to work now. I just said NO!"

You can be in recovery, doing fine, going to support group, taking your meds, and one night you "use" in your dreams. The booze, the needle, the pills, inhaling that smoke, behaving in ways that dull the pain...

It almost works, every time.

Waking in a cold sweat from a drug dream, at first you believe you've slid once more down that slippery slope. That same old familiar, sickening self-loathing soaks through the sheets.

Loser. Hopeless. Weakling.

Drug dreams are part of recovery and they are terrifying. Often they're just terrifying enough to keep you sober. Or not…It's like the brain is trying to switch over to a new way of being, yet there is still the memory of what we were like in that painful unconscious state.

Drug dreams are not just about drugs, either. They're about any destructive behavior that keeps being repeated, despite negative impacts on life and relationships.

I started wondering why I was having these dreams, in which I was my old self, screwing up over and over, leaving a trail of destruction behind me. Was I questioning myself about whether I was healthy now and could live a new life?

…Because it's been many years since I lived those in those old ways…and maybe my dreams are showing me the frightening mess of how I used to live to give me a fresh perspective.

Everything that's happened to me is part of who I am. I can't change the past, but I can change the present and maybe the future.

Pain is not to be forgotten. It's to be integrated. Life changes us.

I'll never be the same.

And thank God for that.

—— TRAINSPOTTING ——

Like the 1990s film about heroin addiction, squalor, poverty and urban decay were all right before my eyes when I took the train to Vancouver recently. Trains are a unique way to travel because their path cuts through a hidden wasteland, seldom seen from roads and walkways.

Garbage-strewn strips of gravel, old mattresses, tires, faded keep-out signs and people tucked into small places. It's familiar to me, from my time on the streets, and I shudder, knowing how it is to intentionally hide like that, tunneling into brambles, safe for a short time, while it lasts. Only my quickly passing eye on the train spots them.

Vancouver is thought of as a "beautiful" city and it is that, with mountains, sea, beaches and a vibrant cosmopolitan vibe. More and more towers crowd the West End and especially lower Davie and Pacific, where there is no end to things for young hipsters to spend money on.

Meanwhile, like something other than humans, outcasts on the sidewalks are ignored by the quickly walking, well-dressed privileged with cell phones glued to all their parts that register other beings.

I grew up there, scrambled on those streets, but this is not my town anymore.

Eaton's has been replaced by a super-sized, full-on, glitzy Nordstrom, with a new "open" floor plan and brighter lighting so everyone can see everyone. Its atmosphere is more like a casino – frenetic, buzzing and conscienceless. The place is packed with people, all clamoring for something to buy that will give them meaning, power, distraction or a pause in their self-loathing. The air tingles with a frantic desperation to consume.

And right outside the shining glass doors, our own refugees challenge us to spot them in plain sight.

An Easter Sunday Miracle

I hadn't been to Saint Andrews Cathedral for five years, ever since I was baptized there, which at the time had freaked out a few friends and made a couple of my old Catholic Aunties back east very happy. For some reason, though, on this bright, blossom-filled Easter Sunday, I just woke up and decided to go to church.

I put on a pretty dress, tamed my hair and set off for the Cathedral, getting there in perfect time, with the eleven o'clock crowd just flowing in the doors. Father John was greeting people. He saw me and gave a nod and a smile, looking happy to see me after so long an absence.

"Hi Father John! Happy Easter!" I smiled back, then quickly crossed myself with holy water and looked around for a seat, but I couldn't see an empty pew anywhere. The cathedral was already full, with hundreds of well-dressed people crammed in, all waiting for the service to begin.

Valerie, who was a faithful regular there, spotted me and came running up to hug me, gushing that I was "back!" and "Praise the Lord you have returned to us!" I told her I was just "back" for the day, but that it was good to see her.

"Ooooh, I wish you could sit with me up in the third row, where we always sit," she said breathlessly, "but there's no room. We're packed in like sardines!"

"Oh, that's okay. Thanks Valerie. I'll find a spot and see you later," I said, feeling good that she'd thought of me.

Another woman waved to me from the middle of a row, right near the back, picking up her coat and squeezing her husband over to make a place for me. She patted the seat beside her with a saintly smile, happy to do a good deed, so I gratefully sat down.

Just as I was settling in to look at the hymnal, I glanced up to see Valerie frantically walking down the aisle, scanning the crowd. Then catching my eye, she yelped above people's heads, "Come over here, dear Rebekah. We made a spot for you. Please join us up at the front. Quick! Hurry here before the service starts…"

I apologized to the nice lady and her husband, then followed Valerie to my plum spot up front in the third row.

It seemed I was destined to sit there.

Catholic mass is a lot of work. Not only do you have to know all the right things to say in response to what the priest says, but you have to stand up, sit down, kneel down and do all this several times throughout the hour or so of the service.

I was enjoying every bit of it today, even more than I'd remembered: the singing, the incense, the prayers, all the voices. A feeling of bliss was humming in my chest, like some familiar song.

Then everything started to move very slowly.

Father John was saying the Eucharist. He was holding the symbolic body of Christ above his head, up to the heavens, saying, "Lord, I am not worthy to receive you. Only say the word and I shall be healed."

But I knew I was worthy, that everyone was worthy.

My eyes must have been shut, because now I noticed they were open and I was standing with the congregation. Everyone was standing, everyone except the frail old woman in the pew directly in front of me. She didn't move.

It was, no doubt, my years of paramedic training that made me reach forward and tap her on the shoulder, leaning over to say in her ear, "Are you okay Dear?"

She wasn't okay. Her chin was down on her chest and when I touched her cheek, it was ice-cold. My fingers went to her neck and her carotid pulse was absent. I caught her under both arms as she slumped over.

The lady next to her swung around and gasped, "Oh my God!"

"Quick, grab her legs and lay her down on the seat," I said. "Call an ambulance right now!"

Leaning over the pew, I locked my lips on her icy, wet mouth, gave her a couple of breaths and started doing chest compressions. Surreal, bizarre and absolutely weird as it was, there was nothing else I could do.

Even weirder, the service kept going.

With so many people there, even Father John couldn't see what was going on at first, but when he did, he swooped down with his holy water and started doing the last rights on the lady.

"Stop!" he told me. "Don't touch her."

I ignored him, not about to stop doing compressions. Father John prayed, I kept doing CPR and suddenly, she grabbed my wrist, and with her blue eyes staring straight into mine, she said, "I'm okay!"

Father John and I both froze and looked at each other, then he stopped what he was doing and ran back up to the stage to try to get the holy service back on track.

Some other people had gathered around us, a woman was propping her up, giving her a drink of water, and a bunch of young girls were standing around crying and praying. Others were kneeling in the aisle, crossing their chests and I was sitting with my head in my hands.

Just when I thought things couldn't get any stranger, the side doors of the church swung open, sunlight poured in and the paramedics rushed to the front with their stretcher. One of the crew was Wayne, someone I'd worked with when I was with the ambulance service.

"Rebekah!" Wayne said, surprised to see me. "What are you doing here? What's going on?"

"Well, the lady went into arrest and I did CPR on her, then Father John came down with the holy water and she grabbed my hand, said I'm okay and now here she is," I stuttered.

"Rebekah, can't you stay out of trouble for one minute?" Wayne said, smiling. I tried to laugh, but couldn't. The room was spinning.

Wayne and his partner lifted her onto the gurney, rolled across the front of the cathedral, back out through the side doors and they were gone. The service continued, incense, singing, Hail Marys and all, just like nothing had happened.

I think the fact that the show kept going was even more bizarre to me than a woman rising from the dead during Easter Sunday service.

I didn't mean to upstage anyone...

We had holy communion, ate and drank Christ, then Father John said a couple of words about "the commotion up front," explaining that a lady was ill and had been taken to hospital, but he said nothing about the Easter Miracle that had just taken place!

Had I just imagined the whole thing? The service was over. I was standing there, feeling kind of light-headed as I turned to walk down the aisle.

As I walked, I heard people saying, "Thank you, thank you, thank you." Someone called me an "angel." I kind of felt like throwing up.

My skin was all goose-bumpy and cold. I snuck out the side door to my car and drove home, feeling like I'd been in a dream.

When I got home, I called my then boyfriend (now my husband), Sinan, and told him I wanted to Skype right away so I could tell him the story. He cried, which I thought was a very appropriate response. I was crying and laughing too.

Sinan later told me that he'd recounted the story to our friend Michele, who had been raised Catholic. Michele protested loudly that Father John's delayed and low-key reaction to the event was because it was a woman who'd fallen ill and a woman who was caring for her. She was sure that if it was a man, the priest would have called out, "He is risen!"

I've done a lot of CPR in my time, but nothing like this had ever happened. People in cardiac arrest, especially older folks, do not spontaneously come back to life. When the heart stops beating, it most often does not start again not without a lot of advanced cardiac care, like drugs and defibrillation and even then, it's very rare for the heart to recover its regular rhythm. In this case, there was no defibrillator, no drugs, no fancy gear, just the basics of human care, with a pinch of the divine.

Later on, I emailed Father John, trying to make sense of it all.

His reply was priceless: "Thank you for what you did for our dear parishioner. Without your help, the outcome would no doubt have been much worse. She is in hospital doing fine now and I went to see her later on to give her holy communion. Her husband and sister, who were sitting with her at church, are very grateful to you. Thank you again for your quick action. I also like to think God had a hand in things today. Praise the Lord. He works in mysterious ways."

For sure Father John. We were a great team. You with the holy water and prayers, me with a bit of CPR, and the Lord making sure we both did his work. It was an Easter Sunday miracle.

Give Me Shelter

We split into two groups, armed with flashlights and maps of the area. We begin walking in the dark, looking for people sleeping outside, in vehicles or makeshift shelters. I've done the homeless count before, though tonight I feel exceptionally lucid and present to the task. There is a definite déjà vu to this evening for me.

I've been here before, walking past houses whose warm lights shine inside, apart from me. I am just a stranger and not welcome in there. I remember being scared as a teen on the street, looking for anywhere that signaled a refuge, somewhere safe for me to close my eyes to the peace of sleep.

Sometimes I'd try a garage door, and if it opened, there might be a place in a corner to curl up for a time. Maybe a basement door was unlocked and no one would hear me if I laid on their couch…I took these risks, even hoping to be caught by someone kind who'd tell me I could stay. Feeling alone and desperate drives one to do unusual things.

We walk past vehicles and look for which ones have steamed-up windows and other signs that someone is inside. Cars and vans were a favorite place I used to sleep. I'd try the back door of a van to see if it was unlocked. Many times there'd be blankets and a foamy, or if not, the floor was fine, too.

A few times I was asleep and the person got in their vehicle, then noticed me when they put the key in the ignition. I'd have to run like hell. I lived like an alley cat…

We walk up a slippery concrete stairway with wooded areas on either side, shining our flashlights into the brambles, peering into the darkness, listening. A man's cough somewhere in the dense brush tells us someone is there, so we back out, leaving him in peace. He must be living in those woods. Is he alone? It's so dark, muddy and cold. My spine tingles with some old memory. We count, "one."

Another man ambles towards three of us standing together at four in the morning under a streetlight. He's slowly walking, seemingly gauging if we are friend or foe. He gets closer and says hello as he keeps going past, then we see him sit in a dark stairwell. Maybe this is where he'll catch a bit of rest. And knowing we are not people who will hurt him, he can close his eyes for a while. Tonight at least there's no rain so he can rest in peace without a shelter over his head.

Under the Magnolia Bridge, Seattle

A few minutes later we drive away and I wonder if he'll get up and keep walking, having lost us as his sentry. The sun will be up soon anyhow and soon I will be safe in my own bed, sleeping, but not this man.

Where will he go? What will he eat? Who cares about him? Who can he talk to? Where is his family? How did things get this way?

When I was a homeless teenager, shelter and food were essentials that I learned to get however I could, even trading myself for what I needed, just to live.

I was telling my friend Carrie how when I was homeless and hungry, I'd find someone to buy me a meal, knowing there was a cost. "Did you have sex with them?" she asked.

"Yeah, some of the time, that was the only currency I had and I used it to survive," I told her.

"Did they give you money?"

"No," I said. "I never asked for money."

"But you could have made a lot of money if you wanted to…"

"Ha! Yeah, maybe," I say, wondering out loud. "Maybe…"

OTHER

The more we find that we have in common with someone, the more we feel a sense of kinship. In fact, when we want to be close to someone, one of the ways we do this is to look for commonalities. By focusing on what is the same, we create bonds with one another.

Conversely, when we want to be separate, when we've decided we do not want to be aligned with someone, we look for what is different. By focusing on what is different, someone becomes "other" and we are separate and isolated from them. They are not "one of our kind."

What would happen if, just for one day, we looked for what we share in common with each person we saw? Would they become more human to us? Would we feel better about the world and ourselves in it?

Stability and Housing for Everyone

A young pregnant woman came for acupuncture treatment today, looking distressed. She said she'd been having headaches, nausea and anxiety and she wasn't sure why. "I just don't feel stable," she told me. "I feel scared and shitty and I want to feel settled and excited about my baby."

After I asked a few questions about what was going on in her life, she told me that their rent had just been raised $400 a month, her hours had been cut to half time at work and her husband had to move his job to another city, making for a longer commute every day. I echoed to her that all the changes must be difficult, when she really just felt like putting down roots and making a nest for her baby. "Yeah, I want to feel stable. I want to feel safe," she said softly between tears.

Under the Magnolia Bridge, Seattle

We talked about the affordability of Housing and she told me that their balcony was too rotten to stand on and the building was falling apart. Because of the raise in everyone's rent, six families were moving out at the end of the month. "But we're staying for now. We have to," she said. Advocating for people to have affordable housing is part of how I spend my time and in moments like this I wonder if anyone in city hall is listening.

One time my husband and I were marching on Martin Luther King Jr. Day in a crowd of thousands downtown carrying signs handed out by organizers, with an image of MLK and quotes from him about peace and unity.

A thin and poorly dressed man yelled at us as we crossed the street, "Hey! You two look like you have a home. What are you doing here?"

Not missing a beat, my husband answered back, "We're marching because we believe everyone should have a home!" The man smiled, waved and kept on walking. I wondered if he had a home, somewhere to feel safe and stable…

—— HOUSING IS HEALTH CARE ——

Sometimes I hear people talk about "The Homeless" like they are another species, rather than fellow human beings who do not have a roof over their heads. In fact, there is such division, such an inability to relate to people who are un-housed, that they are treated with disdain and even contempt. Why?

I serve on the Planning Council for Seattle-King County Healthcare for the Homeless. We meet once a month to help policymakers develop new and better ways for people who are poor and may not have housing, to gain access to healthcare resources. These people are young and old, veterans and civilians, single people and those with children, and many of them have health issues directly related to not having a stable, safe place to live.

At our last meeting someone said, "Housing is healthcare." The statement hit me right in the heart. Without housing, all our efforts to care for people who do not have a home to come to each night, to sleep in safety, to wash and take care of their bodies, to cook meals and sit down to read a book or watch TV, to raise children who feel hope for their futures, is just a band aid on a gaping wound.

Housing is healthcare. We all deserve a place to live.

The Gift

One of my family members was diagnosed with multiple myeloma in 2011. He's had a bone marrow transplant and ongoing rounds of chemotherapy for these past five years, which have kept him alive. I've admired how he carries on living, going to Mexico with his wife, visiting with the rest of the family, playing guitar, riding his bike and just being his usual dependable solid self. When we were there recently, he was building a cedar strip canoe and volunteering at the local hospital thrift store. No moss grows on that guy.

We were talking about my work and he was asking about what I meant by "integration of trauma and loss." I started explaining about how when difficult things happen in our lives and when we can fully integrate pain into who we are, what seemed like something horrible transforms into something else.

"For instance," I said, "With what I imagine has been incredible difficulty you've been through with your cancer diagnosis and all the treatment over the years, you seem to have found a way to live with and accept your illness. You seem to be doing fine, in spite of it all."

He paused, just long enough for me to feel uncomfortable, then said: "You know, it hasn't been hard for me at all. When I got the diagnosis, everyone was in shock, crying and all, and I just felt…joy. It was joy and relief because I had been so unhappy with my life and I knew that I'd been secretly asking for something to come along and change everything, and here it was, my cancer diagnosis, my gift."

I was my turn to pause. I sat there humbled, letting sink in what I'd assumed about him, never having really asked how it was to experience living with cancer. "So is that integration, do you think?" he asked.

"Um, for sure. I understand more now how the process is so different for everyone. Your integration was immediate, it was true acceptance. It's a remarkable thing."

"Yeah, I'm a pretty lucky guy."

"Yes you certainly are. Wow."

—— STABILITY ——

Stability is enduring. When something is stable, it endures regardless of outside influences. Stability is not static and rigid, though. Rather, when something is stable, it is also flexible and fluid. This sounds contradictory, yet stability is only stable when it includes the unknown. As the old saying goes, "The only thing constant in life is change."

Can I be comfortable with the unknown? What is stable in me right now? What can I always rely upon to be here in my experience, regardless of circumstances? What does the deepest, most stable, enduring part of me feel like? Can I tune in and notice it right now? What is always present? What has always been present?

—— WE NEED THEM ——

When we experience the trauma of loss, devastation, violence, abuse, neglect and all the other difficult experiences in our lives, something certainly changes in us. Most people would say that the most likely response is to close down and become more isolated, turn to addiction, inflict violence on others. In fact, this is more the exception than the rule. Yes, hurt people hurt people, but not all people who have been hurt lash out to hurt others. The majority of people who experience extreme tragedy go on to live, informed by something which touched them deeply. Their hearts have been broken open.

There are a lot of people in our world right now who have no place to live. Many thousands are displaced by war and they travel treacherous mile after mile, with babies on their backs and no food or water, to get to a safer place. This is not new. It has been continuing, unabated in one country or another for decades, while those of us safe in our warm beds with full bellies cannot imagine the struggles, dangers and terror they go through.

Today I was discussing this with a patient lying on the acupuncture table during a treatment. I said to her, "I bet those poor people coming from Syria could teach us a lot about what it feels like to carry on with such heartache and still keep living. They can still feel gratitude, see a life ahead and try to make new plans. We have a lot to learn from them. We should let them in."

"Yes," she said. "We need them here."

Indeed. We can learn from their generosity and resilience. We can learn how to open our hearts and welcome people who are homeless in our own country and from abroad. We need the people from war-torn countries like Syria, as much as they need us, maybe more.

☯

···· XIN XUE ····

In the relatively small city of Victoria, there are four schools of acupuncture and Chinese medicine. Ours was known as the hippie school, painted pink on the outside, funky and homey on the inside. Our teacher, Doctor Wally Mui, was the owner of the International School of Traditional Chinese Medicine and a fifth generation doctor of TCM.

Dr. Mui taught us to do qi gong, an ancient martial art used to center and calm energy, before we worked in the student clinic each day. He made us meditate before working with patients, sometimes saying to one of us, "You are not calm enough to put needles in. You sit longer. People who come here are sick. They need to feel welcome, for you to be kind to them. You sit until ready."

During the SARS outbreak in China and parts of the West, he made big batches of special herbal anti-flu preparation for all the students to drink. We'd all sit in the chilly classroom, clutching our mugs of dusty-tasting tea, feeling nurtured by how he cared for us.

When any of the women students in our childbearing years started looking pale, he'd say, "You go see Doctor Jenny (his wife) to give you acupuncture treatment to open four gates and get some herbs for your blood. Heart is fire element. Do not get too excited all the time, or you hurt your heart. Stay calm, grounded. You live longer that way."

Dr. Mui

There were so many small things that Dr. Mui did for us, like on Chinese New Year, he'd give each student a red envelope with a dollar inside for good luck. At noon break, Wally liked to walk down the hill to Chinatown with a dozen or so students for lunch at the Ocean Garden Restaurant, where he was a regular, impressing us with ordering exotic foods for us to try, sometimes food not even on the menu. Then often he'd just pay for all of our lunches, laughing and saying, "I had a good night at casino. You are lucky today!"

He taught us the classic ways of handling, weighing and packaging all the raw herbs in our dispensary, always joking with his dry wit and wry smile: "This one good for growing hair. See I don't take enough of it. I need to drink more tea!"

I asked him one day in class, "Dr. Mui, how did you decide to practice acupuncture and Chinese medicine? Did your father tell you to? Or did you just decide it was what you wanted to do?"

Doctor Mui paused for a moment, then said, "For generations, traditional Chinese medicine has been practiced by my family. It is our xin xue (pronounced "shin shway"), which means our heart blood. When something is your heart blood, there is nothing more important to you. It is your life. Without the heart, the blood could not move in the body and without the blood, the heart would be empty."

Doctor Mui passed away recently, but his words still ring in my heart. Thank you for showing us your xin xue every day, dear teacher. I will try to be this kind of practitioner, too.

. . . .

—— DISCERNMENT ——

Judgement comes from our thoughts about the world around us and ourselves in it. Ideas and beliefs we've "installed" in our minds and our beliefs can seem so real that what we construct becomes our "operating system" and life is created, based on what we believe. The tighter we cling to our perceptions, the more we feel the need to "protect" and "defend" our position. We are at war with whatever does not agree with us.

Discernment is something different. Discernment sits quietly in the background, noticing the ebb and flow, not needing to drop anchor in the depths. It's a radical way of being that says, "I don't know. But I am curious and willing to find out."

Feeling Welcome

Some people just have a way of making you feel welcome. It's the way they smile, ask you about yourself, want you to be comfortable and just generally help you feel relaxed, like you're in the right place with the right people.

Today marks six years that I've lived in the U.S. and I have to say that I have felt very welcome here. I was a little afraid, moving to a new country, starting all over with my business and making new friends, but I have more close friends who say, "I love you!" to me now than I ever have in my whole life. I say it more, too. Saying I love you feels good.

Besides all the loving friends I know in Seattle, I got the chance to go to my husband's thirty-fifth high school reunion in the Midwest a couple of summers ago and meet a whole new crowd there. Because they love my husband, they made me feel welcome with their smiles and questions about myself. They hugged me, told me I was "one of them" and basically took me in as an honorary classmate. I was stunned by the flood of generosity and kindness. I'd never had a high school reunion, let alone a real high school experience, but here it was, thirty four years later!

After the reunion dinner my husband said, "Well, did you have a good time?"

"At least six people told me they loved me," I blubbered. "They don't even know me and they love me!"

"Of course they do," he smiled. "You're in Iowa! That's how people are here."

Almost seven years of love and welcome is something to celebrate. Thank you my American friends. I love you, too.

Chairs

Funny for me to get sentimental about chairs. But here I find myself on this fragrant spring evening, thinking about chairs, feeling their presence. Funny, to be so sentimental. It must be the wine…

A good friend came by this morning with some chairs in the back of his truck. He'd come by for a visit and as he was leaving, said as an afterthought, "You guys don't need any lawn chairs do you?"

"Sure," my husband says, always wanting to add to the collection in his man cave.

"Are you sure? Cause they're really old. But Cindy's grandmother had them and she was attached to them, for all the good times spent sitting and visiting in these chairs…"

"Rebekah! Do you want these lawn chairs?" husband calls out.

"Yeah!" I say, looking out and seeing the first one in the herb garden, basking in the sunshine warming its frayed slats. "Yeah, I like them!" I say, noticing something, though I'm not sure what, which tells me these chairs and I have some sort of destiny.

Funny to be so sentimental…about these chairs.

My dad had an old chair, a Lazy Boy recliner, like most dads had. It was orange velour, stained on the arms from so many long hours in front of the TV. The cats scratched it often, stretching up as far as they could reach, to get their claws in deep to mark where they, too, liked to sit.

His chair sat by the front door, where he'd look across the lawn to the Fraser River delta, maybe dreaming of better days, of what could have been done differently…

I'm pretty sure his chair was a sort of refuge from the world, a place to relax and let go of the day. It was his place to feel good, his throne.

Facing south, sunlight flooded our living room when the front door was open. The smell of new-mown grass and blossoms on a spring evening wafted freshness into stale corners of our house. A rare, bucolic, carefree sweetness came right in on the breeze to my dad in that chair.

Except for Dad and the cats, no one else sat in the chair. It was somehow understood, just like Archie Bunker and his chair...

These four chairs, being lifted out of the truck, had stories to tell of laughter, trust, friendship, forever promises, dreams. They are full of love.

And I am so funny, to be so sentimental about chairs...

I went outside and picked up the first chair, placing it on the wood chips by the hedge, facing east. Sitting down on it, I closed my eyes, imagining the morning sun in that spot. The next one went a little further back, in the garden, where I knew the late morning sun would land, by the rhubarb patch. The next chair would catch the strong southern light; the last one I put by the plum tree, facing southwest, to get the last rays of sun before it goes behind the trees.

The cat and I sit in the southwest chair this evening, soaking in the warmth, me with a smile and glass of wine, having just eaten a salad with my garden gifts of kale, green onions and sorrel. Both our eyes are slitted to the last of this day's light. Her fur is warm. My hand is melted to her back.

The chairs are at home here and I am happy they have accepted their new place with us, somewhere else to feel the love of people who sit in them.

I'm so funny, to be so sentimental like this. It really must be the wine...

—— SLEEP ——

Sleep is meant to be a time when our minds can let go and allow the nervous system's gas pedal to release and the brakes to slowly be applied, so we can awaken feeling refreshed. As a child, my sleep was often disturbed by what I could hear going on in the house. I felt afraid and I was plagued for years with frightening dreams and my health suffered from improper sleep.

The dreams have mostly gone, though sometimes my nervous system still has difficulty ratcheting down to where there is nothing more to do when I lay down to sleep but allow surrender. Over the years, with mindfulness practice plus lots of help and grace in life, I have learned to let go and fully relax, which gives my nervous system a break, teaching it to become more flexible, restoring choice. Interesting, how letting go helps restore our ability to choose to sleep, which is the ultimate in letting go.

Shoulders and Acceptance

I injured my right shoulder a long time ago. It could have been a fall off a motorcycle, tree planting on the coast, arm wrestling contests with loggers at the bar, or showing off in push-up contests at parties on Hornby Island. That's what we did for fun, at least it's some of what I did when I was twenty-something and thought I was invincible.

It could have been the years of hauling stretchers up and down stairs, not to mention deadlifting two hundred or more pounds in and out of the ambulance (before today's much easier-on-the-body "self-loading" gurneys), or even all the teaching demonstrations of CPR over thirty plus years.

What wrecked my shoulder could also have been years of farming, digging, throwing around ninety-pound bales of alfalfa, fifty-pound sacks of grain, wrestling and shearing sheep, baseball, tennis, golf, swimming, martial arts…I did all of those things like my life depended on it and every day my body, not just my shoulder but my whole body, lets me know that I could have been a little kinder to it, a little more gentle.

Lots of us have pain and even more once we hit the fifty-year mark.

Fortunately, with age comes, hopefully, a bit of insight or wisdom to adjust activities to those that are easier on the body, but more importantly, to see what else we do that gives us pain. That's what I was hoping for.

I've been paying close attention to my neck and shoulders these days trying to notice exactly what is happening in my body when I am uncomfortable. What position am I in? What am I thinking? What emotions am I experiencing? Am I tense? Relaxed? Am I in this present moment with my thoughts or am I miles ahead of myself? Especially in my neck and shoulders, these observations are not only relevant, they reveal how much pain comes from my habitual patterns of thoughts and nervous-system responses.

I did a one-week silent Zen meditation retreat last spring. I'd done several retreats before and I sit every day for at least half an hour or more, so I felt comfortable with the five or so hours we'd be sitting every day in forty-minute segments. I won't say it's ever been easy for me, though I've definitely learned to sit through my discomfort to the point where it eventually gets better. But not this time.

I was fine when I got to the retreat, so where was this insane pain coming from? The intense burning pain lasted most of the retreat, despite my willingness to "surrender" to it, which was really just another strategy I desperately used, trying to make it stop. I popped Ibuprofen, did yoga, lay down as much as I could, prayed, breathed and basically just kept on doing whatever I could to escape from the pain. Nothing worked.

On the last day I was so exhausted and numb from not just the pain but from all the emotions that surfaced when I was faced with just sitting and not doing anything. Not only did my whole body feel the repeated surges of my nervous system's habitual forward movement to escape, but something in the background was patiently noticing every twitch of my mind and each time the programmed response to regain control – by changing the breath, the thought, the position I was in – failed to ease my pain. No matter how subtle my attempts, every strategy I tried was on display, like I was watching a movie.

And the pain suddenly stopped.

The lesson I learned was that even when I thought I was being gentle with myself, my inner taskmaster was actually in control and when I became aware of that, everything softened. Now, almost daily I have a smaller, less intense version of pain, noticing, trying to escape from it, then letting go, because there is nothing else to do. And my hands also tell me a story by their clenching and releasing with my thoughts, so here, too, I can learn to surrender my "grip" and relax a little more.

My shoulders are just one of the paths to acceptance of what is.

THE TAO AND
···· MODERN MEDICINE ····

East Asian medicine originates from the study of nature. Thousands of years ago people in China who lived simply and in harmony with nature were said to be "Taoists," those who followed "the way."

Yin and Yang and the Five Elements of wood, fire, earth, metal and water are the central concepts and are the basics of how Chinese medicine works. Each element has a season, color, emotion, organ and many other associations connected to each element, all based in nature.

The season of late summer sits between summer and autumn. Late summer is when heat changes to moisture, plants begin to bear abundant fruit, rotting and softening begins. It's the time of the spleen and the stomach's functions of digestion are at their peak. The color is yellow. Spleen season's emotion is worry, which tells us that to worry excessively will hurt our digestive process.

Biological science shows us that worry does in fact cause a release of more cortisol into the bloodstream, which has an adverse impact on the stomach and small intestine, where the bulk of our digestion takes place. Excess cortisol, the stress hormone, breaks down the immune system, part of which is the spleen, the producer of many of the infection-fighting white blood cells we need to combat disease. So yes, worry hurts the digestion. How'd they know this, two thousand years ago?

Interesting how such old "folk medicine" is interfacing more and more with modern western science. As someone who began my medical background with emergency care, moving to mental health and then on to East Asian medicine, I see how it's possible for all practices of healing to combine and inform one another in harmony, giving us the best ways to care for body, mind and spirit.

The Tao is still "The Way."

Hot Flashes

Our bodies never lie. Sure, it seems like sensible, folksy logic, but then when we get sick, or some strange thing is happening to us, we feel suddenly betrayed by our body, like we might have done something wrong…Hey! Whatever I did, I didn't mean it and besides, you were supposed to be my friend!

WTF?

Mom never told me about hot flashes. Maybe it wouldn't have changed a thing, but now I wish she had told me a bit about what it was like for her to move beyond her childbearing years. I wish I'd had more direct knowledge of this little detail of womanhood. Even with all I've read and heard from my patients about their sleepless nights and sopping days at the office, I had no idea how it would be.

Now it was my turn to steam and I was unprepared for the all-encompassing immersion into this sweltering rite of passage.

This is what it's like: Suddenly, when it seems like you are minding your own business, usually when you are trying to do something important, requiring your full concentration, the mysterious volcano within begins to boil. It is invisible, except to the trained eye of another menopausal woman, who sees the droplets on your upper lip and notices that you are shedding layers of clothing, looking for an open window.

Nights are another thing altogether. Thrashing, kicking, I twist in the wet sheets, lost in chaotic dreams, running and thirsty, always thirsty.

I stopped counting one day after the twenty-fifth hot flash and decided to apply what's always helped me in times of distress: giving bare attention to my whole self, trying to notice the source of my discontent.

I watch every thought, breath and movement in the moments before a hot flash flares, which means, since I never know when one will come over me, I end up focused even more than usual on watching myself.

Do I get a hot flash when I am anxious? How could it be that even in the morning, all alone, six o'clock, just me and my cup of tea, birds chirping merrily, cat stretching out on the rug in a sunbeam—I start to slowly broil. There is nothing to be anxious about. Yet, I feel the heat building like a candle has been lit in my chest, spreading now like a wildfire.

Is that where it starts? Is it in my chest? Or does it start in my scalp, now wet, or my lower back, also soaked?

If this is giving you a hot flash, I apologize. And if it's any consolation, I gave myself a hot flash too, just writing about it. But, in a few minutes it's gone and now I feel normal again, like nothing ever happened.

Nothing to see here folks. Move along.

I went to see a naturopath who does homeopathy, having done all the things that I'd used to help other women with their hot flashes, but getting nowhere with myself. No coffee, no wine (oh how I missed a glass of wine but it was shown clearly to make matters worse), and just trying to be "good" wasn't working.

"What's going on for you when you flare up?" she asked me.

"I think I'm not in the present when I get a hot flash. It's like I want to be somewhere else, other than where I am right now and I start to burn up."

She was good, getting this clarity from me right away. I trusted her and went on to talk for an hour-and-a-half about my whole life. Being born, living as a child, a teen, an adult, my beliefs, what I regretted, what I was proud of, the trauma, the joy, the stupid things, the desperate things I'd done to escape something – myself.

Escape myself. It's futile. I'm just spinning my wheels, burning rubber.

And now my body was telling me to let it all go; to let go of trying to be somewhere other than here and now. There is no escape.

It's a deep pattern I've been seeing for some time now, when I sit quietly each morning. My body subtly leans from right to left in an almost imperceptible rotation, like I could jump up and run right now if I had to. There it is. I see my nervous system, the unconscious ways I think. This is how I've gotten used to living, in the next moment. In a future that doesn't yet exist.

So when the pattern arises, my body notices and responds. It thinks I am a gazelle running from a lion. But that is just an old response to feeling unsafe.

It might be my imagination, but I think I am more patient these days, more carefree.

Que Sera Sera...

Just knowing what triggers my hot flashes helps them become less frequent and even less severe. I've had five hot flashes today so far. Each one informs me that there is only now.

My body won't let me forget that for a minute.

—— OUR BODIES SAY NO ——

A patient came for acupuncture treatment recently with some pain and other complaints he thought might have been related to his sports activities. He had a several issues with muscles and joints, as well as signs of an overactive sympathetic nervous system.

We talked about his sports activities as well as his high-stress work in the corporate world. He spoke of his way of approaching things in a very analytical way, which was the style he was accustomed to, feeling that by using his brain he was able to "make informed decisions" based on the data collected. When I asked about his sports and how those things might be connected to his pain, he pushed aside the idea that his activities were in any way contributing to the issues with his body, which was strange, because he'd come in talking about just that.

As a holistic practitioner, it's my job to look deeper into what is on the surface, to find the "root" of the problem so it can be treated, as well as the "branch" or manifestation (i.e., the symptoms of the ailment). So as I began needling, I started asking more questions, to see if we could open up more in the conversation and reveal some answers.

I knew it was important for me to be gentle and allow him to speak, while reflecting what he said. We are living in a society where we associate being "right" with being "safe," so when people feel challenged to see things differently than the view they have held, they can literally feel under attack and I wanted him to let down his guard enough to allow for more personal insight.

"This pain and twitching seem to just come randomly. There is no pattern. It doesn't make sense. I'm not a super athletic guy and I sometimes can't do what other people can do."

"I bet that doesn't make sense to your competitive brain, eh?"

"Yeah," he said, as the last needle went in and he closed his eyes.

"Just try to pay attention to what you are feeling when pain, numbness, twitching or other discomfort comes up," I advised him. "Your body is saying no to something and only you know what it is. It may not be entirely physical. Sometimes how we relate to the world worked great for a while, then it ceases to serve us. I don't know, only you do."

Our bodies are smarter than our brains. I know this from decades of personal neglect of my own needs.

I also know that if we pay attention to thoughts and habitual ways of feeling, we can learn what messages our nervous systems are sending us. And then we can respond sensitively to our needs, like the aching shoulder, the sore back, the stiff neck, digestive issues... Our bodies are speaking to us and they want us to listen.

This is how we learn to love ourselves, starting right here, right now.

"It Doesn't Affect Us"

What we humans are being forced to understand is that we all breathe the same air.

Nothing we do is in isolation from the rest of existence. Mathematician and meteorologist Edward Lorenz was a pioneer of chaos theory. Investigating the way small things can have large effects later on, he was able to notice how even something as small as a butterfly's wings moving, could alter weather patterns thousands of miles away. In fact, even the tiny changes a butterfly's wings might make in the air could ultimately change the path of a storm, or even prevent a tornado from happening in another location. Hence, the phrase "butterfly effect" became a common metaphor, used both in and outside of the scientific literature.

Small things can make a big difference…

Sitting down to dinner with some folks, the conversation turned to the latest in politics. A certain candidate's name came up and a young girl about age thirteen said she was "scared" of that person getting into office. Her father held her protectively close, saying "Don't worry Honey. We're safe where we are. Even if he gets in, it doesn't affect us."

The young girl didn't look convinced and went back to staring at her cell phone.

"We are all affected by everything," I started to say as my appetite left me. "Racism, classism, sexism and anything that hurts people, erodes our society, our world. It matters to all of us. Everything we say and do matters." I felt sick now, wanting to run.

The table went silent and everyone kept eating. I could feel eyes on me. The air was sticky and cold, but I wasn't sorry that I spoke out. I'd stifled the urge to say much more…

Many years ago my Pentecostal pastor father wrote a book called *The Rapture and The Mark*. Most evangelical Christians believe that one day, when we least expect it, Christ will call his chosen people to come up to heaven to be with him, and everyone else will be left behind. The biblical quotes scared me: "In that place there will be weeping and gnashing of teeth when you see Abraham and Isaac and Jacob and all the prophets in the kingdom of God, but yourselves being thrown out."

Gnashing of teeth.

"It will be sudden," my dad told us. "Suddenly, some people will just disappear and be taken up into the sky to be with the Lord."

Even as a kid, if I'd known the word "Bullshit" I would have yelled it out at him.

I'd challenge him, "But what about everyone else? What about all the nice people and animals who don't go to church? What about people who have never heard of Jesus, who live in the jungle or up on mountains? What about people who are poor and can't get to church? Where will they go? Will they get hurt? Doesn't Jesus care about everyone?"

Patting the top of my head he'd usually say something like: "We will be safe. What happens to the others is not our concern. They should have loved Jesus and now they will have to pay the price. Don't worry. All that matters is that we will be with the Lord."

This is when I would have used my choice word: Bullshit.

"I'm not going! God is mean!" I'd wail. Looking jumpy, angry and another emotion I hadn't seen that often, he'd pat my head some more.

"We are protected because we are his children."

"No one will ever read your book about Jesus coming and only taking good people. It's stupid."

Silence.

Ah. Separation. The thing we keep doing, thinking it keeps us safe, when all it does is take us away from where we started and where we eventually end up, once again, scattered particles of light.

Who would think we'd be so afraid of that? But we are.

Every single breath every single one of us takes, matters. Every kind word, or unkind word, every thought, every drop of water, gallon of gas, affects us all.

All the systems that imprison people, marginalize and exclude people, hurt people, animals and plants, affects us all.

I knew it then and I know it now. Insulation eventually breaks down and all we're left with is who we are.

Like it or not. We are all in this together and no one gets out alive.

—— CHANGING OUR MINDS ——

We get used to behaving in certain ways and others get used to expecting the same type of responses from us, the same opinions, the same likes and dislikes. Then every so often we might surprise people, even ourselves, by doing, saying or believing something different. Sometimes, we change. Sometimes other people change, if we can allow them to be different in our minds. Or we can continue to hold them in the same judging light and see how that feels.

We might not even know whether a person is "a certain way," or maybe it was just a friend's opinion and we "adopted" it as ours. Bit by bit, our world gets narrower because we have closed a part of our mind and heart to a person or a whole group of people, maybe even a whole race or country or gender of people. We miss the beauty when we hold so tightly to our judgments. It hurts.

But there's always the opportunity to change our minds. We can stop right in the middle of spouting an opinion and say, "Actually, that's not true for me anymore. I feel differently now." It might be hard to get the words out, but then suddenly there's space and freedom. A new world opens up to include more people.

As the years go by, stopping in my tracks, even mid-sentence, is a more and more common occurrence for me. I feel both ridiculous and liberated when I take the step to change my mind and let down my walls to the world. And it's worth it every time.

Sabbath

Today I sat outside with my cat in the sun doing not much of anything. We soaked up the precious warmth of early fall light, sliding into the hammock as the sun shifted, then to the grass, where she perched on my chest, both our eyes happy slits, blissfully smiling in the rays. I'd caught a bit of a cold in the last day or two, so the sun's heat felt healing, like it was baking the chill right out of me. Laziness can feel almost sacred at times.

My husband had been looking forward to a day like this for quite a while. His birthday was yesterday and so from sunrise to sunset today he invited me to join him on a "Sabbath" day of rest. We planned to loosely follow the traditional way of keeping the Sabbath, with no work, no computers and no travel, staying at home in our own backyard. We made a fire in the pit and cooked a late lunch on the embers (though, as the good book says, "you shall kindle no fire… on the Sabbath," so we did take a small liberty with that). We talked, read, did a crossword, played guitar. I even sang a bit in a croaky, sore-throat voice. "We should do this every week."

"I know, eh?" I said. "It's like camping. I like doing nothing."

It's so simple, but actually, doing nothing takes commitment, too. Having no barriers like computers, cell phones, TV and other electronics to interfere with our intimate, relaxed talks was my favorite part of today.

I was reminded of my three years living on an old wooden boat on the north coast of BC—silent, reflective, renewing and simple. I never missed having a TV and we didn't even have personal computers and cell phones in those days anyhow. My entertainment was reading or dropping a line over the side to jig up some cod for dinner.

Now the sun is down but sweet Sabbath has taught me to remember the importance of taking time to stop for another day of rest soon.

——— SILENCE ———

We say we want it, but we do everything to distract ourselves and avoid silence. I'm not speaking of when we stop talking and the TV is off, because the noise keeps going in our heads unless we make time to notice the space when silence is bigger than sound.

Philosopher Friedrich Nietzsche called sitting and noticing silence, otherwise known as meditation, "mental hygiene." I love that, mental hygiene, so we can purge our minds of all the detritus in the way of clear spaciousness.

Spiritual teacher Adyashanti calls meditation "the most sincere form of prayer" and "pure receptivity." How often are we purely receptive? Can we learn how to be more receptive by focusing more on the present moment?

I'm told by people much wiser than I, that just "noticing" moments of silence is important to reinforce it in us. Sometimes we can notice deep silence at the oddest times...

I was outside on a summer evening with my cat after dinner, the sun was warm on both our backs and her eyes caught the light as she gazed at me. Silence filled all space and everything disappeared for just a minute or so. Then my thoughts began again.

Her Eyes

He took her eyes. Of all the things to take from someone, her eyes. And she sat there speaking about "the incident" when someone she'd known, someone she'd loved and cared for, beat her almost to death and blinded her. He knew how precious and irreplaceable eyes are, so that's what he did first. He took her eyes.

I didn't know her but I got the chance to go see her today. When I heard about what happened I knew deep in my guts how it could have been me. She was homeless when this terrible thing happened. It could have been me so many times when I'd been homeless and beaten. But I still have my eyes.

I had to go see her. I wanted to hold her hand. I just wanted to hold her hand. My husband drove me. He wanted to come too.

And where two eyes had been, there were just lids, all swollen and, inexplicably, there was a smile for me, a stranger who was welcomed.

"Come and sit down please. I love having visitors. I'm so glad you came. What's your name?"

I sat on the bed, reached out my hand and we held each other. I held her tight at first, wanting to comfort her for all the hurt. And then my tears started falling as she told the story of what had happened. I leaned in and she cradled my head on her shoulder, being used to comforting people her whole life. She patted my head, "Your hair smells so pretty. Thank you for coming to see me."

"Where is your family? Are your parents coming?" I asked.

"No. I think they're busy or something. It's okay."

"No it's not. It's fucking not okay," I said.

"Yeah, I know," she said, patting my head some more.

"You're safe now you know," I told her hopefully.

"Yeah, life is going to get better for me. I'm looking forward to it. People are all helping me. I'm going to live with other blind people. It'll be good."

"You're amazing."

"Yeah, I'm a miracle. I died and they brought me back. I'm a miracle."

We left and returned a few minutes later with a bag of Nacho Cheese Doritos and a Dr. Pepper, because she'd told us that those were her favorites. When I came back in the room there was a friend visiting and they were laughing and she was holding the little doll I'd brought her.

Broke my heart and made my day.

Yes you are a miracle darlin'. You truly are.

TRAUMA, ACES,
——— HOMELESSNESS AND LOVE ———

ACEs stands for Adverse Childhood Experiences study. It's a well-known tool, used by health professionals, social workers and other social-service providers to assess how difficult childhood experiences may be impacting their clients.

The questions ask about adverse events happening before age eighteen, like parents divorcing, substance abuse and mental illness in the home, family violence, etc. The more points you score, the more likely it is for you to be impacted by addiction, poverty, violence, incarceration, chronic health problems, to name a few.

The relationship between childhood trauma (as measured by ACE scores) and chronic health problems has captured the attention of a growing number of researchers. Findings indicate that those with high ACE scores (four and up) are more likely to experience violence and abuse which, over the course of a lifetime, correlate with many chronic health problems (a phenomenon referred to as COLEVA: Consequences of Lifetime Exposure to Violence and Abuse).

In other words, childhood trauma matters, a lot. In his book Zebras Don't Get Ulcers, *Robert Sapolsky explores body/mind research showing the link between early childhood Trauma, chronic stress, high cortisol levels and autoimmune disease. The evidence is irrefutable, yet modern medicine still struggles with the cause of so many diseases and too often medicates, rather than listens.*

The research literature also links high ACE scores with homelessness and sadly, but predictably, finds that those who've already had a hard start in life are much more likely to become homeless.

In one research study, more than 85% of homeless respondents reported at least one of the ten adverse childhood experiences and more than half (52.4%) experienced more than four ACEs. More than half (55.1%) suffered the loss of a biological parent before the age of eighteen and a similar number reported a lack of family support growing up (51.9%) and living in a home with a substance abuser (50.3%). More than half of respondents (51.4%) report having experienced verbal abuse and 22.2% report that they did not receive proper care growing up. More than a third (40.5%) of Homeless respondents suffered physical abuse by a parental figure. Over a quarter (29.7%) had a sexual-abuse background.

I did the ACE survey and found I could check off more than half on the list of ten questions regarding things like parents divorcing, sexual abuse, violence, mental illness in the household, a family member in prison…

And my childhood is a walk in the park compared to what some people faced as children and still face every day as adults.

ACEs is not an exhaustive list. Whatever is interpreted by a young, developing person as feeling unsupported, unprotected and lacking nourishment, in short, feeling un-loved, can have adverse effects and repercussions down the road.

In other words, love matters, a lot.

And knowing that love matters, we should have a pretty good idea of what is needed to make things better in our world. All good things grow out of love.

Like my friend Susan says, "love wins love."

Mother's Day

I don't ever remember seeing a photo of her when I was growing up. My brother sometimes drew pictures of her, a big round ball of scribbled blond head on a stick body with red lips. His pictures always made her look wild and angry, yet that was not how her memory lived in me.

The warmth of her embrace…her voice, a clucking monotone of small details…"Let's get your arm in the sleeve…good girl…just another spoonful…looks like you're full…good girl…"

She lived in my body, in my cells. My hands were her hands. My baby finger curved just like hers. I knew these things because when I looked at my dad, I did not see myself in him. I must look like her then. I was created in her image.

At school I used to say she was dead. It was easier than trying to explain what I didn't understand myself, that my Mom left one day and never came back to live with us. I felt ashamed. So on Mother's Day, when kids at school asked about my mom, I just said, "My Mom died." That way no one would ask any more questions.

I'm pretty sure the teachers knew my parents were divorced and my mom was not dead, but for whatever reason, they didn't say anything. Looking back, that seems very respectful of them, just letting me be with my grief, even if I was lying.

I had no reason to feel shame that my parents were divorced and my Mom was gone, but shame is what I felt, like she'd left because of something I did, or something I was.

Shame turned to a slow simmering rage and I hated her for the chasm she left in my life. Nothing and no one was out of range of my bitterness.

That's what happens when love festers. It turns to poison.

And there was no denying the rage I'd carried inside me, at my father for driving my mother away with the abusive and cruel treatment of everyone in our family, and even for sparing me from it.

As the odd one out, I unwittingly became a witness to the crimes, not even knowing what I was actually witnessing, forced to absorb the sticky guilt, as my father's favored child.

Favoritism became my cross to bear. I still feel it sometimes, the burden of being the only one not beaten or sexually abused by him. Then, being a witness to my father's treatment of my brother Michael, seeing how he became emotionally crippled by the rape of his innocence and crushing of his self-worth, I didn't know how else to cope, except to pull inward and hate myself.

Being a survivor when others are in ruins is a two-edged sword which can continue to damage with guilt and shame and can also provide distance from the trauma for perspective and even healing... But that takes time and lots of other ingredients.

Then there was my brother David, so full of talent, sparkling with life, so loved by Mom as her first "baby boy." He spent most of his life, from the time he was sixteen, behind bars, where whatever secret shame he harbored over what happened to him as a child never saw the light of day. Instead, he was filled with hatred and spite until his early death.

My sister, who left home as a teen, like I did, lived with neighbors and married for the first time at age sixteen, just to get away. She moved to California, trying to distance herself from the legacy of a toxic family; she has survived and even thrived, but not without the struggle to shake off her early childhood trauma and negative self-image.

Mom in the '60s

But even more than my father's crimes against his wife and children, it is what my mother did, and didn't do, which has caused me to question not just my worth, but my very right to exist. A mother reassures her child that they are safe and not alone. That is really a mother's sole job. And that didn't happen, not for a very long time, until after I squeezed it from her. Then, finally we healed all that shit, together.

My father, after all, was the one who kept me housed and fed through my childhood, in between his raging and abuse, at least doing some of the basic things a parent should do. My mother, on the other hand, fled, for good reason, I will agree, and even attempted once to return and take us with her, but after that she did not even try, for many years, to be with her children.

Instead, she later bragged to me about all the "fun" she'd had all those lost years of my childhood, travelling, having "lots of boyfriends" and living life like she didn't have two young children, because, she didn't. I had to bite my tongue when she'd talk about the good times she had and was still having, without the responsibility of caring for us.

And when I was fifteen, with nowhere else to go, I desperately needed her to be a mother to me. But when I came to live with her, she lost patience after a few weeks and put me back out on the street again to fend for myself.

One day, when we were talking on the phone, I was brave enough to bring up the subject of how it was for Michael growing up and how he still suffered as an adult, from the childhood sexual abuse from our father.

"Why didn't you do anything?" she said.

"What are you saying?" I asked. "I was a child. How could I have helped? I didn't even know what to do!"

Then it struck me. I spoke slowly. "Mom, did you know my dad was like that? Did you know he was doing those things? Was he doing those things before Michael and I came along?"

"I didn't know what to do either," was all she said.

I hung up the phone.

So there it was: the abuse, the helplessness, the complicity. I couldn't speak to her for months after that, trying to process the ugliness. This one was going to take a while...

I never had kids myself. Damage and scar tissue from too many bad things happening to my body gave me another reason to be bitter. And I was bitter, like the taste of bile when nothing else is left.

I'd been married the first time to a good man who would have been a good father if we'd had children. I thought having kids would be how I would redeem my family's terrible past. "Someone's got to do it right," I said flippantly to one of my aunts. I was sure I'd have twins too, like my brother David's wife did, and like in Mom's family, where among her twelve siblings there were three sets of twins.

But that marriage failed. I failed it, because I was broken and foolish and dishonest and still hated myself.

And amazingly. It still amazes me. Many years later, a year after Mom died, when I had reached the milestones of completing both my counseling and acupuncture degrees, and was finally starting to find some inner peace, I met Sinan at a five day workshop on addiction with Gabor Matè at a retreat center on a BC Gulf Island.

Hollyhock Lifelong Learning Centre on Cortes Island is the kind of magical place where, I always joked, you could "find your soulmate," though that was for other people, the lucky ones, the group I didn't feel part of. But it was where we first saw each other and started a long-distance love affair, with him in Seattle and me in Victoria.

We wrote a lot of long emails, discovering our shared worldview of community, redemption and caring for people. I came to Seattle for a visit and we were married a year later.

To say Sinan is my best friend, lover and partner, is not nearly enough to describe how he nurtures each corner of my soul, finding ways to give me whatever gentleness, goodness and understanding I missed earlier in life. He gets me, more than anyone ever has, and loves all the weirdness in me too, like in the song "Everything" by Alanis Morissette: "You see everything, you see every part. You see all my light and you love my dark. You dig everything…"

Which brings me back to the memories and how I am still processing them, even as I write this. Pockets of understanding and release from the pain often sit right beside the grief and ugliness, so I continue to notice both and try to give them equal respect.

With both of my parents, I had the privilege to be alone with them in their last moments as they died. It was there that I experienced, looking deep into the unknown depths of their souls, that they were only human, just like we all are.

My dad's last words were, "Hello! It's so good to see you!" It was as if he was greeting an old friend and I can only hope that in his next life, if there is another chance for him, he can make a new start and do things better the next time around, if there is a next time….

It's not that I have it all figured out, not by a longshot, but as time goes on, I am able to understand more about Mom's bitterness, her withholding of affection, her stinginess with offering praise, with listening, with giving her precious attention and time. I got so little, but I can see how she was folded in on herself and so was I.

There was never enough time for us until she had the stroke and then there was nothing but time, for me to cut her fingernails, massage her hands with lotion ...

At first I was never doing it right, then slowly, over those last years we had together, she stopped complaining, stopped directing, and just allowed me to care for her.

The air became sweet.

"Look how our hands are so much the same," she'd say.

"Yes, I can hardly tell our hands apart."

"No one cuts my nails as good as you do."

"Thanks Mom."

About the Author

Rebekah Demirel is an acupuncturist and clinical counselor, living in the Seattle area with her husband, cat and two chickens. She writes, gardens, sings, dances, works out at her karate dojo, and delights in sharing her healing and insights with the world.

Rebekah's personal belief that nothing and no one is beyond redemption is at the core of her trauma-integration training workshops, where people are guided to cultivate self-care through body, mind and spirit awareness, so they can be "well enough to do the job" of caring for others.

Photo Credit: Rex Hohlbein

www.traumaprograms.com

Made in the USA
Lexington, KY
10 September 2017